KITTY DOODLE

Name & Age:

Address:

Phone & Email:

INSTRUCTIONS

LIST or DRAW Eight THINGS
That you want to learn about:

1.

2.

3.

4.

5.

6.

7.

8.

Action Steps:

1. Go to the library or bookstore.
2. Bring home a stack of at least EIGHT interesting books about these topics. Choose some that have diagrams, instructions and illustrations.

Supplies Needed:

You will need pencils, colored pencils, pens, markers and a new set of smooth black drawing pens for picture study and art exercises.

Choose Eight Books To Use As School Books!

1. Write down the titles on each cover below.
2. Keep your stack of books in a safe place.
3. Be ready to read a few pages from your books daily.
4. Complete 10 pages each day in this workbook.

Circle Today's Date

January
February
March
April
May
June
July
August
September
October
November
December

1 2 3 4 5 6
7 8 9 10 11
12 13 14 15
16 17 18 19
20 21 22 23
24 25 26 27
28 29 30 31

MONDAY
TUESDAY
WEDNESDAY
THURSDAY
FRIDAY
SATURDAY
SUNDAY

2015
2016
2017
2018
2019
2020
2021
2022
2023
2024
2025
2026
2027
2028
2029

Write Today's Date: _ _ _ _ _ _ _ _ _ _ _ _ _ _ _ _

Start Your Day!

Draw Your Dreams:

To-Do List

_____
_____
_____
_____
_____
_____
_____

Practice Using Your Pens

My FUN Page

Picture Study

Look closely at this picture.

Think about the lines and shadows.

Practice working with your colored pencils.

Draw the Missing Spot

Use a variety of smooth black drawing pens,
with fine points, to complete the picture.

Nature Study

Go outside and make a realistic
drawing of something
you find in nature.

Reading Time - 1 Hour (Set a Timer)

Choose Four Books - Read from each book for 15 minutes.

Copy important words or pictures from each book here:

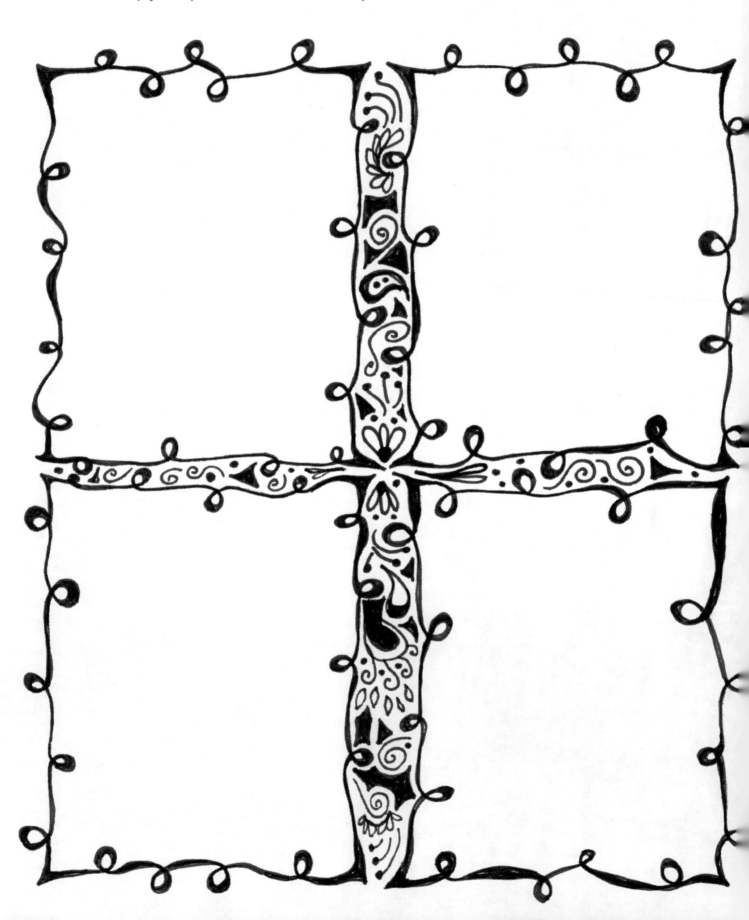

Spelling Time

Find 20 Words with **4** letters each.
Look in your books for words.
Write the words here:

Start Time:

_ _ _ _ _

Stop Time:

_ _ _ _ _

Screen Time!

Watch a Documentary, Educational Program, Movie, or Tutorial.

TITLE: _____

SUBJECT _____

LOCATION: _____

MESSAGE: _____

_____

Rating:

AWFUL

BAD

LAME

YUCKY

OKAY

NICE

GOOD

GREAT

SUPER

AMAZING

Notes:

Draw a Scene from the video:

TITLE:

Use THIS PAGE for Math Practice

Or be creative and design something, like a house! You could make graphs, maps or geometric designs with this graph paper.

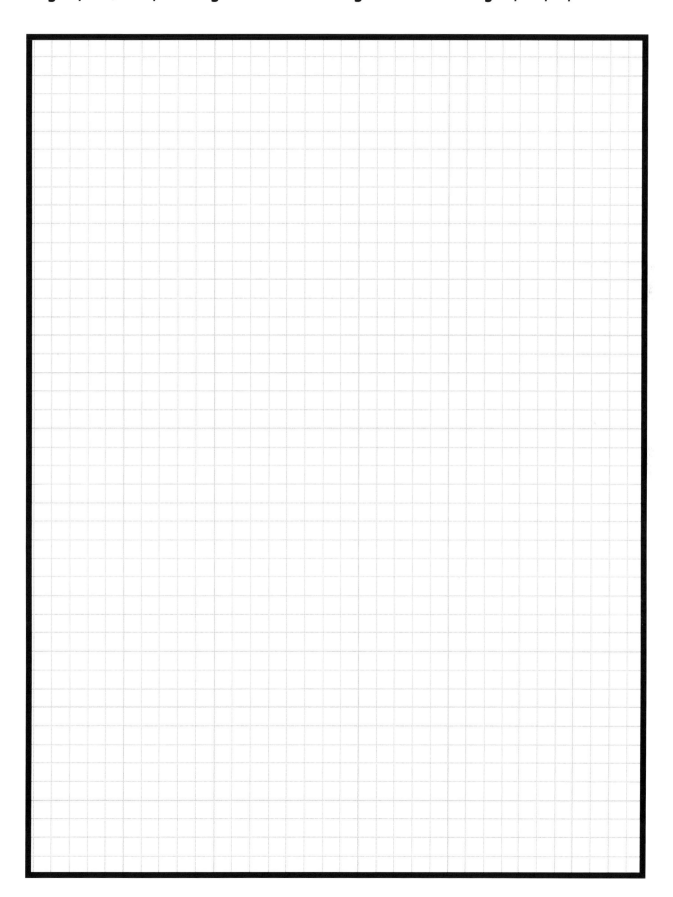

World News Today!

Talk to your parents about current events.

Look at a newspaper, news broadcast or website.

Color the countries you learn about.

Tell the news stories with words or pictures.

Creative Writing & Copywork

Stories, Poems, Lists and More.
That's what this page is waiting for!

_____

_____

_____

_____

_____

_____

_____

_____

_____

_____

_____

_____

_____

_____

_____

_____

_____

_____

Circle Today's Date

January
February
March
April
May
June
July
August
September
October
November
December

1 2 3 4 5 6
7 8 9 10 11
12 13 14 15
16 17 18 19
20 21 22 23
24 25 26 27
28 29 30 31

MONDAY
TUESDAY
WEDNESDAY
THURSDAY
FRIDAY
SATURDAY
SUNDAY

2015
2016
2017
2018
2019
2020
2021
2022
2023
2024
2025
2026
2027
2028
2029

Write Today's Date:_ _ _ _ _ _ _ _ _ _ _ _ _ _ _ _ _

Start Your Day!

Draw Your Dreams:

To-Do List

_____
_____
_____
_____
_____
_____
_____

Circle Today's Date

January
February
March
April
May
June
July
August
September
October
November
December

1 2 3 4 5 6
7 8 9 10 11
12 13 14 15
16 17 18 19
20 21 22 23
24 25 26 27
28 29 30 31

MONDAY
TUESDAY
WEDNESDAY
THURSDAY
FRIDAY
SATURDAY
SUNDAY

2015
2016
2017
2018
2019
2020
2021
2022
2023
2024
2025
2026
2027
2028
2029

Write Today's Date:_ _ _ _ _ _ _ _ _ _ _ _ _ _ _ _ _

Start Your Day!

Draw Your Dreams:

To-Do List

_____
_____
_____
_____
_____
_____

Practice Using Your Pens

Picture Study

Look closely at this picture.

Think about the lines and shadows.

Practice working with your colored pencils.

Draw the Missing Spot

Use a variety of smooth black drawing pens,
with fine points, to complete the picture.

Nature Study

Go outside and make a realistic
drawing of something
you find in nature.

Reading Time - 1 Hour (Set a Timer)

Choose Four Books - Read from each book for 15 minutes.

Copy important words or pictures from each book here:

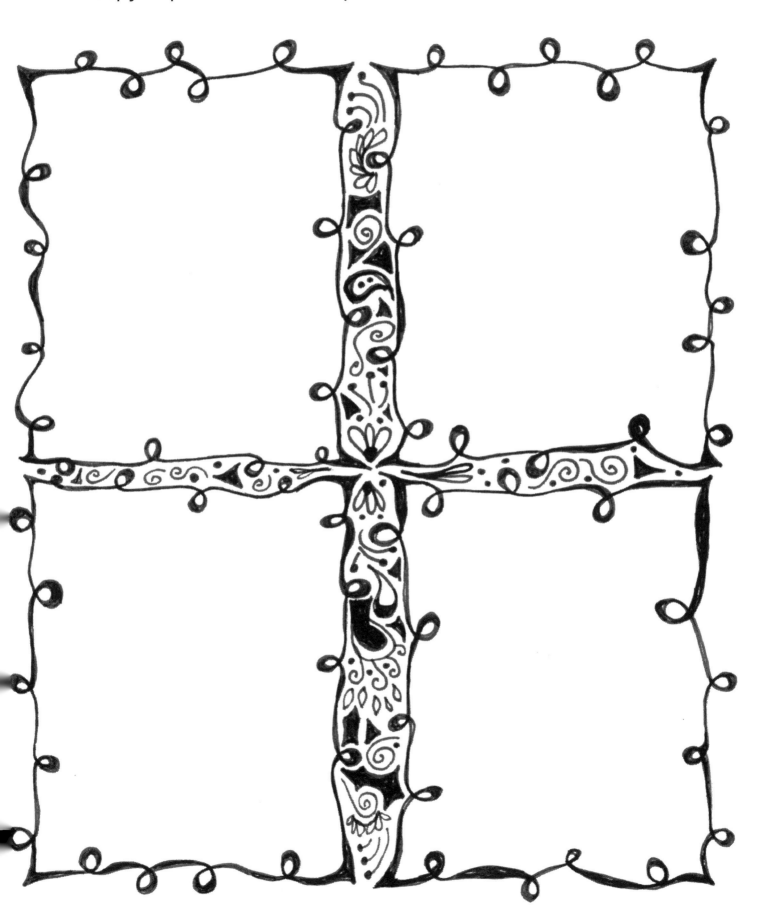

Spelling Time

Find 20 Words with **5** letters each.

Look in your books for words.

Write the words here:

Start Time:

_ _ _ _ _

Stop Time:

_ _ _ _ _

Screen Time!

Watch a Documentary, Educational Program, Movie, or Tutorial.

TITLE: _____

SUBJECT_____

LOCATION:_____

MESSAGE: _____

_____

Rating:

AWFUL

BAD

LAME

YUCKY

OKAY

NICE

GOOD

GREAT

SUPER

AMAZING

Draw a Scene from the video:

Notes:

TITLE:

Use THIS PAGE for Math Practice

Or be creative and design something, like a house! You could make graphs, maps or geometric designs with this graph paper.

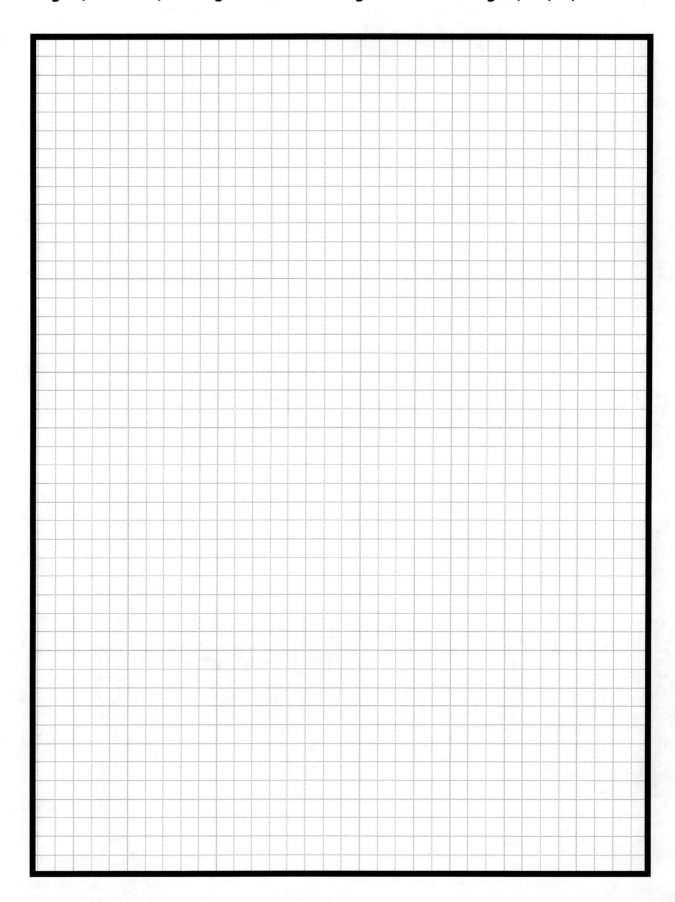

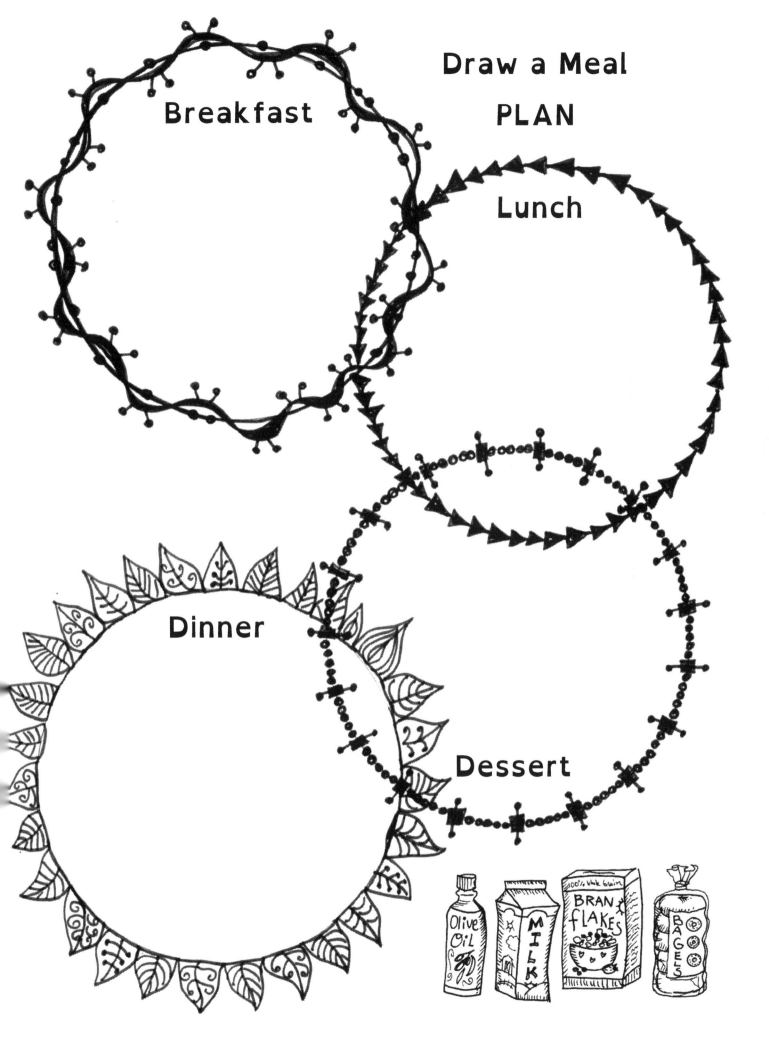

Breakfast

Draw a Meal
PLAN

Lunch

Dinner

Dessert

Creative Writing & Copywork

Stories, Poems, Lists and More.
That's what this page is waiting for!

_____

_____

_____

_____

_____

_____

_____

_____

_____

_____

_____

_____

_____

_____

_____

_____

_____

_____

_____

_____

Circle Today's Date

January
February
March
April
May
June
July
August
September
October
November
December

1 2 3 4 5 6
7 8 9 10 11
12 13 14 15
16 17 18 19
20 21 22 23
24 25 26 27
28 29 30 31

MONDAY
TUESDAY
WEDNESDAY
THURSDAY
FRIDAY
SATURDAY
SUNDAY

2015
2016
2017
2018
2019
2020
2021
2022
2023
2024
2025
2026
2027
2028
2029

Write Today's Date:_ _ _ _ _ _ _ _ _ _ _ _ _ _

Start Your Day!

Draw Your Dreams:

To-Do List

_____
_____
_____
_____
_____
_____
_____

Picture Study

Look closely at this picture.

Think about the lines and shadows.

Practice working with your colored pencils.

Draw the Missing Spot

Use a variety of smooth black drawing pens,
with fine points, to complete the picture.

Nature Study

Go outside and make a realistic
drawing of something
you find in nature.

Reading Time - 1 Hour (Set a Timer)
Choose Four Books - Read from each book for 15 minutes.
Copy important words or pictures from each book here:

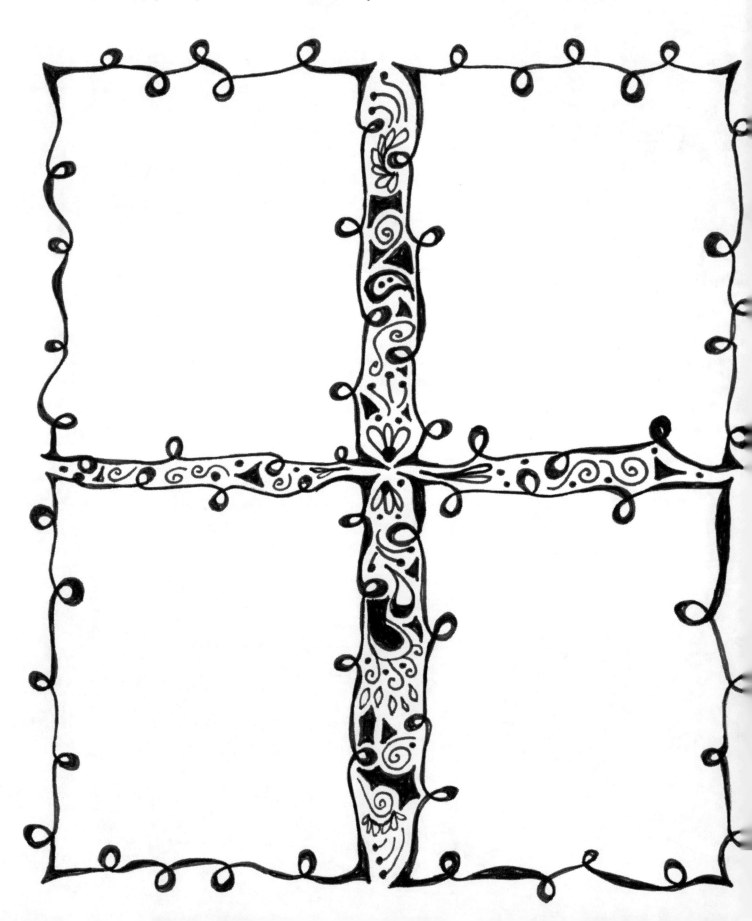

Spelling Time

Find 20 Words with 6 letters each.

Look in your books for words.

Write the words here:

_____   _____

_____   _____

_____   _____

_____   _____

_____   _____

_____   _____

_____   _____

_____   _____

_____   _____

Start Time:

Stop Time:

Screen Time!

Watch a Documentary, Educational Program, Movie, or Tutorial.

TITLE: _____

SUBJECT_____

LOCATION:_____

MESSAGE: _____

_____

Rating:

AWFUL

BAD

LAME

YUCKY

OKAY

NICE

GOOD

GREAT

SUPER

AMAZING

Notes:

Draw a Scene from the video:

TITLE:

Use THIS PAGE for Math Practice

Or be creative and design something, like a house! You could make graphs, maps or geometric designs with this graph paper.

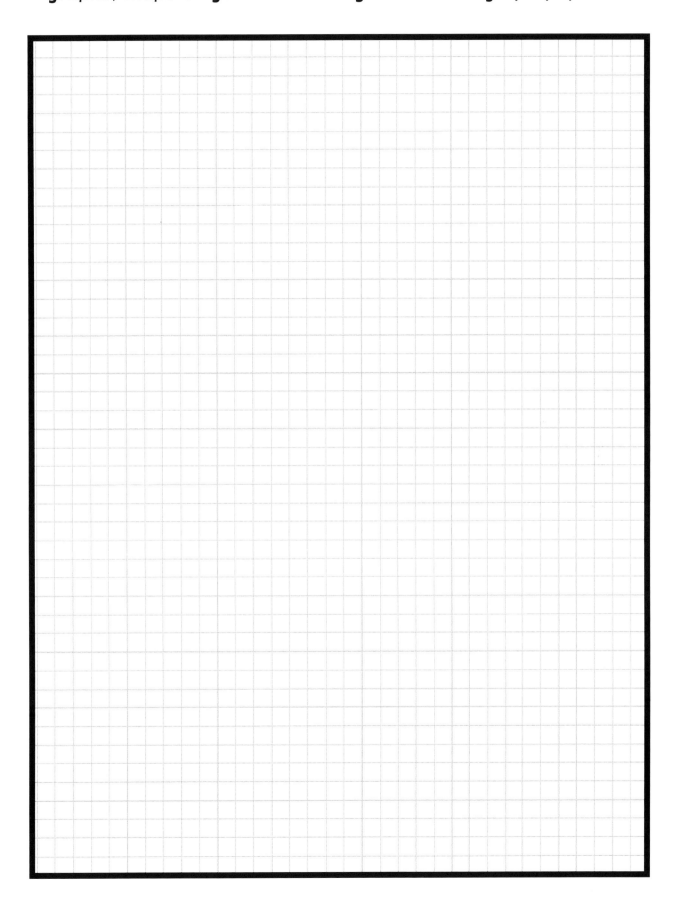

Fun Writing Practice:

ABCDEFGHIJKLMNOPQURSTUVWXYZ

abcdefghijklmnopqrstuvwxyz

ABCDEFGHIJKLMNOPQURSTUVWXYZ

ABCDEFGHIJKLMNOPQURSTUVWXYZ

abcdefghijklmnopqrstuvwxyz

Creative Writing & Copywork

Stories, Poems, Lists and More.
That's what this page is waiting for!

Draw Anything!

Circle Today's Date

January
February
March
April
May
June
July
August
September
October
November
December

1 2 3 4 5 6
7 8 9 10 11
12 13 14 15
16 17 18 19
20 21 22 23
24 25 26 27
28 29 30 31

MONDAY
TUESDAY
WEDNESDAY
THURSDAY
FRIDAY
SATURDAY
SUNDAY

2015
2016
2017
2018
2019
2020
2021
2022
2023
2024
2025
2026
2027
2028
2029

Write Today's Date: _ _ _ _ _ _ _ _ _ _ _ _ _ _ _ _ _

Start Your Day!

Draw Your Dreams:

To-Do List

_____
_____
_____
_____
_____
_____
_____

Practice Using Your Pens

Picture Study

Look closely at this picture.

Think about the lines and shadows.

Practice working with your colored pencils.

Draw the Missing Spot

Use a variety of smooth black drawing pens,
with fine points, to complete the picture.

Nature Study

Go outside and make a realistic
drawing of something
you find in nature.

Reading Time - 1 Hour (Set a Timer)

Choose Four Books - Read from each book for 15 minutes.

Copy important words or pictures from each book here:

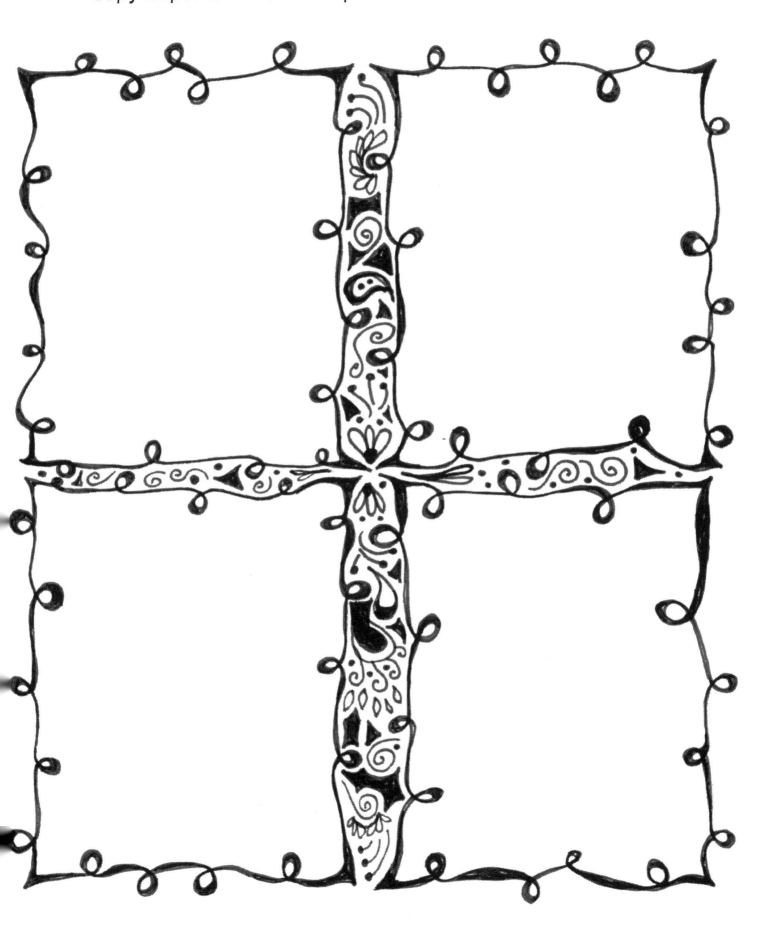

Spelling Time

Find 20 Words with **7** letters each.
Look in your books for words.
Write the words here:

Screen Time!

Watch a Documentary, Educational Program, Movie, or Tutorial.

Start Time: _____

Stop Time: _____

TITLE: _____

SUBJECT _____

LOCATION: _____

MESSAGE: _____

_____

Rating:
AWFUL
BAD
LAME
YUCKY
OKAY
NICE
GOOD
GREAT
SUPER
AMAZING

Draw a Scene from the video:

Notes:

TITLE:

Use THIS PAGE for Math Practice

Or be creative and design something, like a house! You could make graphs, maps or geometric designs with this graph paper.

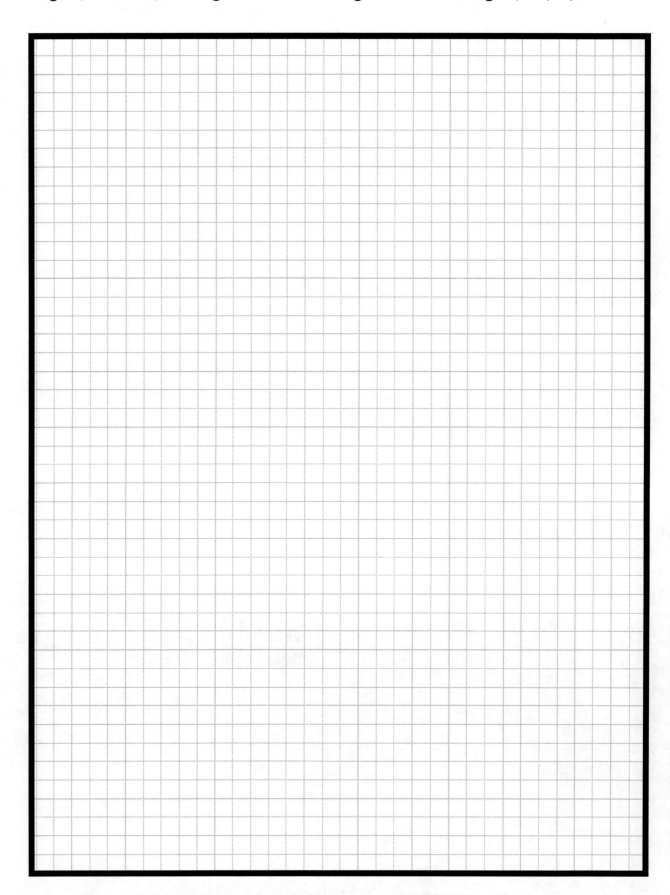

Creative Writing & Copywork

Stories, Poems, Lists and More.
That's what this page is waiting for!

_____

_____

_____

_____

_____

_____

_____

_____

_____

_____

_____

_____

_____

_____

_____

_____

_____

_____

My FUN Page

Circle Today's Date

January
February
March
April
May
June
July
August
September
October
November
December

1 2 3 4 5 6
7 8 9 10 11
12 13 14 15
16 17 18 19
20 21 22 23
24 25 26 27
28 29 30 31

MONDAY
TUESDAY
WEDNESDAY
THURSDAY
FRIDAY
SATURDAY
SUNDAY

2015
2016
2017
2018
2019
2020
2021
2022
2023
2024
2025
2026
2027
2028
2029

Write Today's Date: _ _ _ _ _ _ _ _ _ _ _ _ _ _ _ _ _ _

Picture Study

Look closely at this picture.

Think about the lines and shadows.

Practice working with your colored pencils.

Draw the Missing Spot

Use a variety of smooth black drawing pens,
with fine points, to complete the picture.

Nature Study

Go outside and make a realistic
drawing of something
you find in nature.

Reading Time - 1 Hour (Set a Timer)

Choose Four Books - Read from each book for 15 minutes.

Copy important words or pictures from each book here:

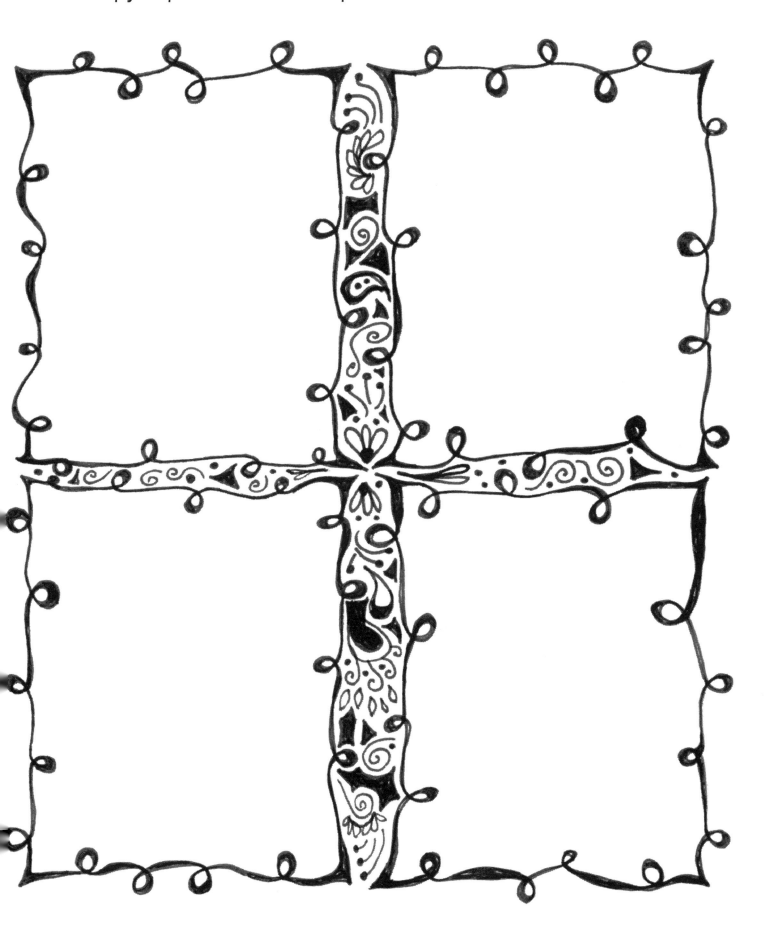

Spelling Time

Find 20 Words with **8** letters each.
Look in your books for words.
Write the words here:

_____   _____

_____   _____

_____   _____

_____   _____

_____   _____

_____   _____

_____   _____

_____   _____

_____   _____

Start Time:

_ _ _ _ _

Stop Time:

_ _ _ _ _

Screen Time!

Watch a Documentary, Educational Program, Movie, or Tutorial.

TITLE: _

SUBJECT _

LOCATION: _

MESSAGE: _

_ _

Rating:

AWFUL

BAD

LAME

YUCKY

OKAY

NICE

GOOD

GREAT

SUPER

AMAZING

Draw a Scene from the video:

Notes:

TITLE:

Use THIS PAGE for Math Practice

Or be creative and design something, like a house! You could make graphs, maps or geometric designs with this graph paper.

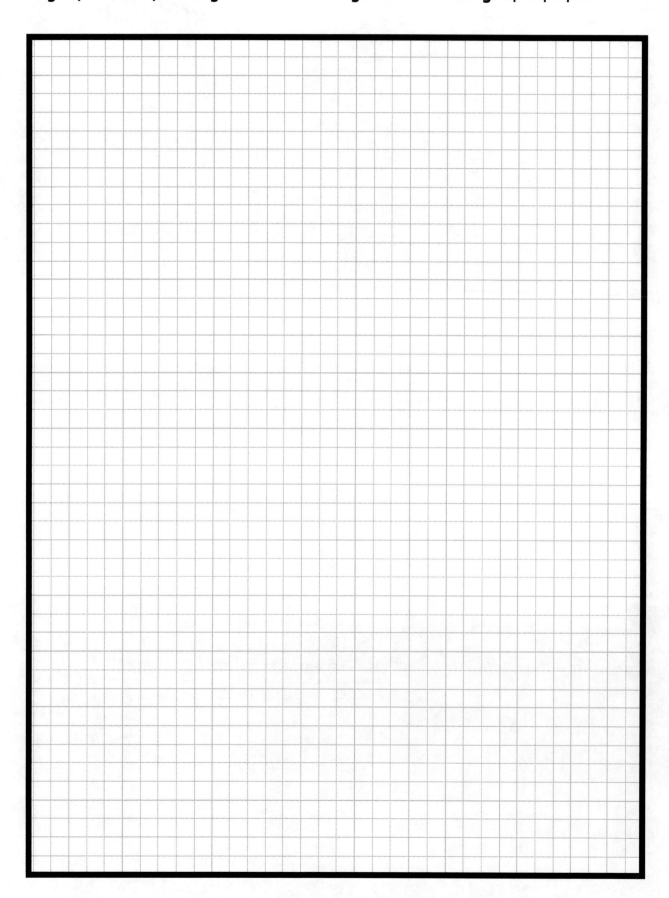

Listening Time

Listen to an audio book or classical music or ask someone to read a story to you while you color and draw on the next page.

What are you listening to?

_____

Circle Today's Date

January
February
March
April
May
June
July
August
September
October
November
December

1 2 3 4 5 6
7 8 9 10 11
12 13 14 15
16 17 18 19
20 21 22 23
24 25 26 27
28 29 30 31

MONDAY
TUESDAY
WEDNESDAY
THURSDAY
FRIDAY
SATURDAY
SUNDAY

2015
2016
2017
2018
2019
2020
2021
2022
2023
2024
2025
2026
2027
2028
2029

Write Today's Date:_____

Start Your Day!

Draw Your Dreams:

To-Do List

_____
_____
_____
_____
_____
_____
_____

Picture Study

Look closely at this picture.

Think about the lines and shadows.

Practice working with your colored pencils.

Draw the Missing Spot

Use a variety of smooth black drawing pens,
with fine points, to complete the picture.

Nature Study

Go outside and make a realistic
drawing of something
you find in nature.

Reading Time - 1 Hour (Set a Timer)

Choose Four Books - Read from each book for 15 minutes.

Copy important words or pictures from each book here:

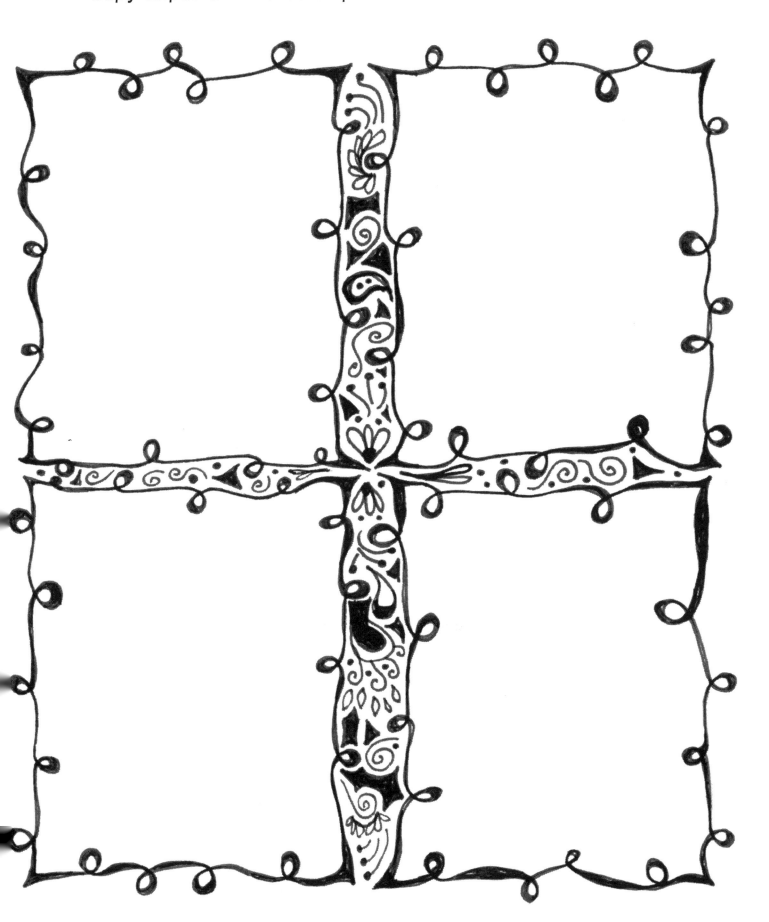

Spelling Time

Find 20 Words with 9 letters each.
Look in your books for words.
Write the words here:

_____   _____

_____   _____

_____   _____

_____   _____

_____   _____

_____   _____

_____   _____

_____   _____

_____   _____

Start Time:
_ _ _ _ _

Stop Time:
_ _ _ _ _

Screen Time!

Watch a Documentary, Educational Program, Movie, or Tutorial.

TITLE: _____

SUBJECT _____

LOCATION: _____

MESSAGE: _____

_____

Rating:

AWFUL

BAD

LAME

YUCKY

OKAY

NICE

GOOD

GREAT

SUPER

AMAZING

Notes:

Draw a Scene from the video:

TITLE:

Use THIS PAGE for Math Practice

Or be creative and design something, like a house! You could make graphs, maps or geometric designs with this graph paper.

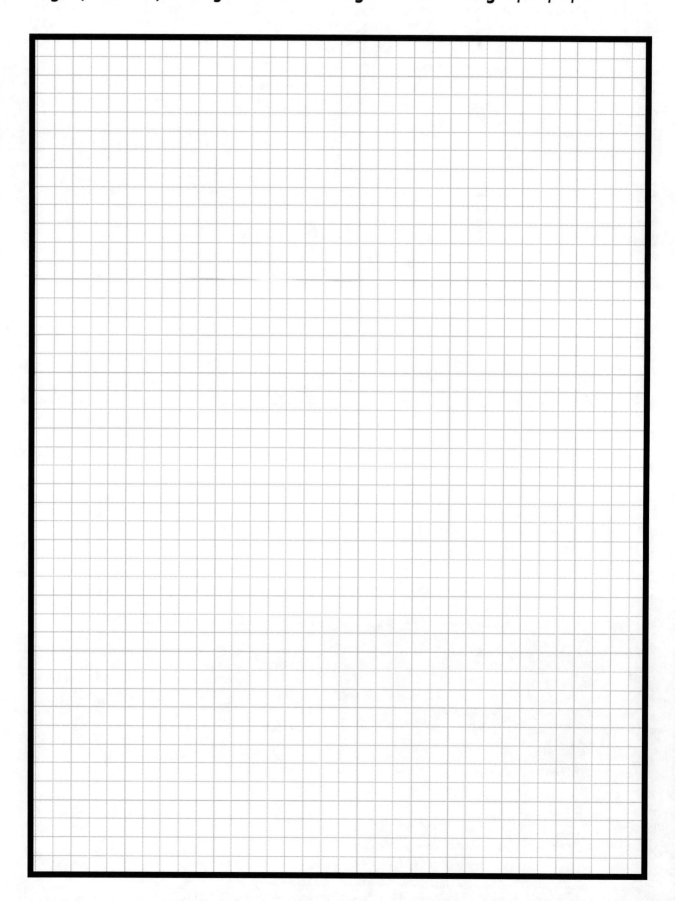

World News Today!

Talk to your parents about current events.

Look at a newspaper, news broadcast or website.

Color the countries you learn about.

Tell the news stories with words or pictures.

Creative Writing & Copywork

Stories, Poems, Lists and More.
That's what this page is waiting for!

_____

_____

_____

_____

_____

_____

_____

_____

_____

_____

_____

_____

_____

_____

_____

_____

_____

_____

_____

_____

Circle Today's Date

January
February
March
April
May
June
July
August
September
October
November
December

1 2 3 4 5 6
7 8 9 10 11
12 13 14 15
16 17 18 19
20 21 22 23
24 25 26 27
28 29 30 31

MONDAY
TUESDAY
WEDNESDAY
THURSDAY
FRIDAY
SATURDAY
SUNDAY

2015
2016
2017
2018
2019
2020
2021
2022
2023
2024
2025
2026
2027
2028
2029

Write Today's Date:_ _ _ _ _ _ _ _ _ _ _ _ _ _

Start Your Day!

Draw Your Dreams:

To-Do List

_____

_____

_____

_____

_____

_____

_____

Picture Study

Look closely at this picture.

Think about the lines and shadows.

Practice working with your colored pencils.

Draw the Missing Spot

Use a variety of smooth black drawing pens,
with fine points, to complete the picture.

Nature Study

Go outside and make a realistic
drawing of something
you find in nature.

Reading Time - 1 Hour (Set a Timer)

Choose Four Books - Read from each book for 15 minutes.

Copy important words or pictures from each book here:

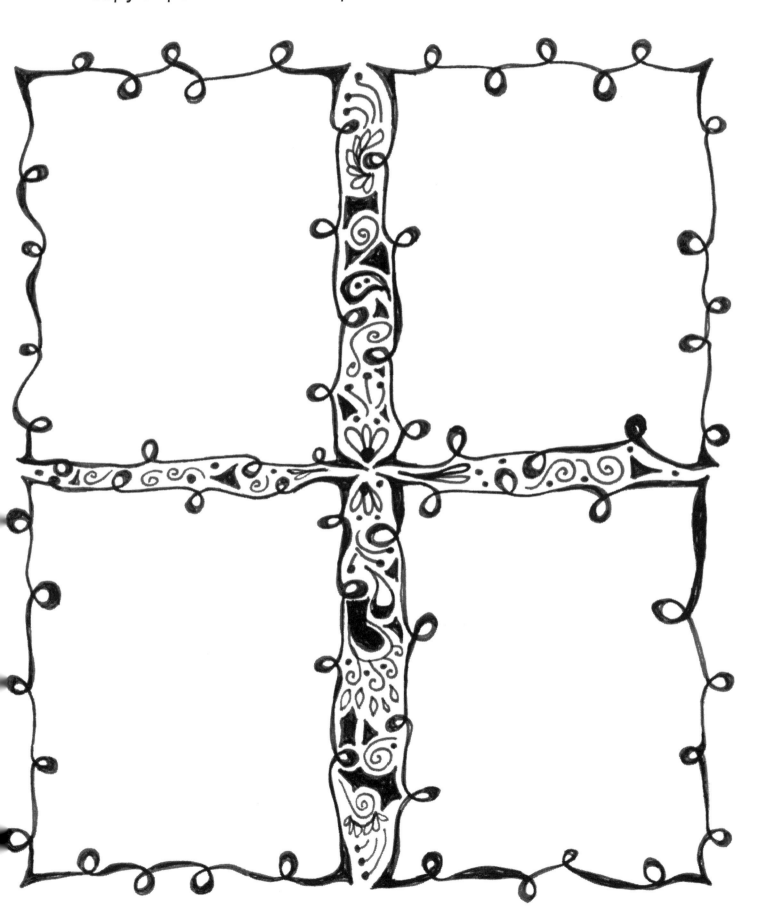

Spelling Time

Find 20 Words with 8 letters each.

Look in your books for words.

Write the words here:

_____   _____

_____   _____

_____   _____

_____   _____

_____   _____

_____   _____

_____   _____

_____   _____

_____   _____

Start Time: _____

Stop Time: _____

Screen Time!

Watch a Documentary, Educational Program, Movie, or Tutorial.

TITLE: _____

SUBJECT _____

LOCATION: _____

MESSAGE: _____

_____

Rating:
AWFUL
BAD
LAME
YUCKY
OKAY
NICE
GOOD
GREAT
SUPER
AMAZING

Notes:

TITLE:

Draw a Scene from the video:

Use THIS PAGE for Math Practice

Or be creative and design something, like a house! You could make graphs, maps or geometric designs with this graph paper.

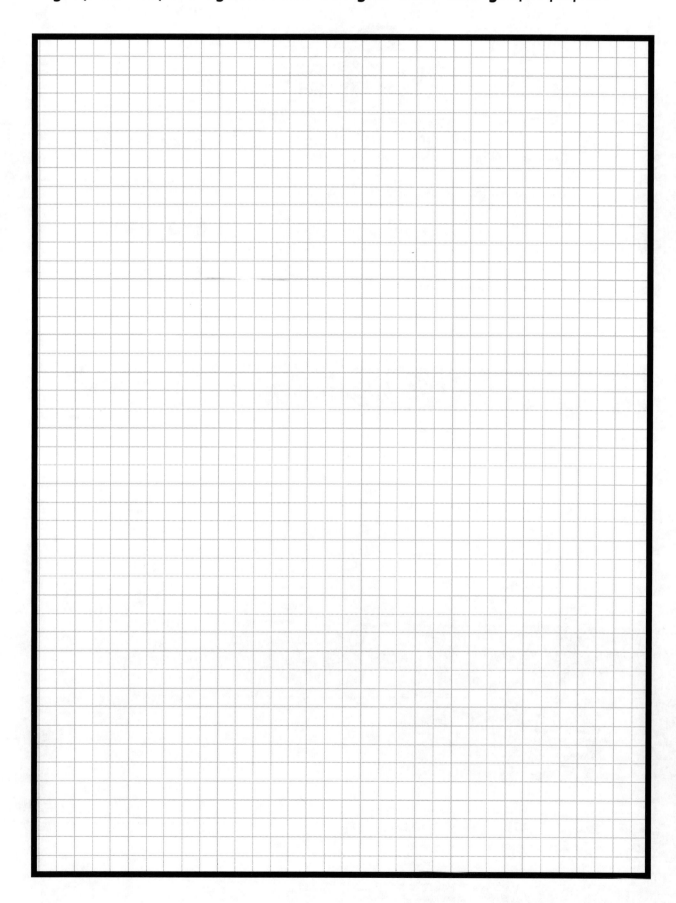

Fun Writing Practice:

ABCDEFGHIJKLMNOPQURSTUVWXYZ

abcdefghijklmnopqrstuvwxyz

ABCDEFGHIJKLMNOPQURSTUVWXYZ

ABCDEFGHIJKLMNOPQURSTUVWXYZ

abcdefghijklmnopqrstuvwxyz

_____

_____

_____

_____

_____

_____

_____

_____

Creative Writing & Copywork

Stories, Poems, Lists and More.
That's what this page is waiting for!

My FUN Page

Circle Today's Date

January
February
March
April
May
June
July
August
September
October
November
December

1 2 3 4 5 6
7 8 9 10 11
12 13 14 15
16 17 18 19
20 21 22 23
24 25 26 27
28 29 30 31

MONDAY
TUESDAY
WEDNESDAY
THURSDAY
FRIDAY
SATURDAY
SUNDAY

2015
2016
2017
2018
2019
2020
2021
2022
2023
2024
2025
2026
2027
2028
2029

Write Today's Date:_ _ _ _ _ _ _ _ _ _ _ _ _ _

Start Your Day!

Draw Your Dreams:

To-Do List

_____
_____
_____
_____
_____
_____
_____

Picture Study

Look closely at this picture.

Think about the lines and shadows.

Practice working with your colored pencils.

Draw the Missing Spot

Use a variety of smooth black drawing pens,
with fine points, to complete the picture.

Nature Study

Go outside and make a realistic
drawing of something
you find in nature.

Reading Time - 1 Hour (Set a Timer)

Choose Four Books - Read from each book for 15 minutes.

Copy important words or pictures from each book here:

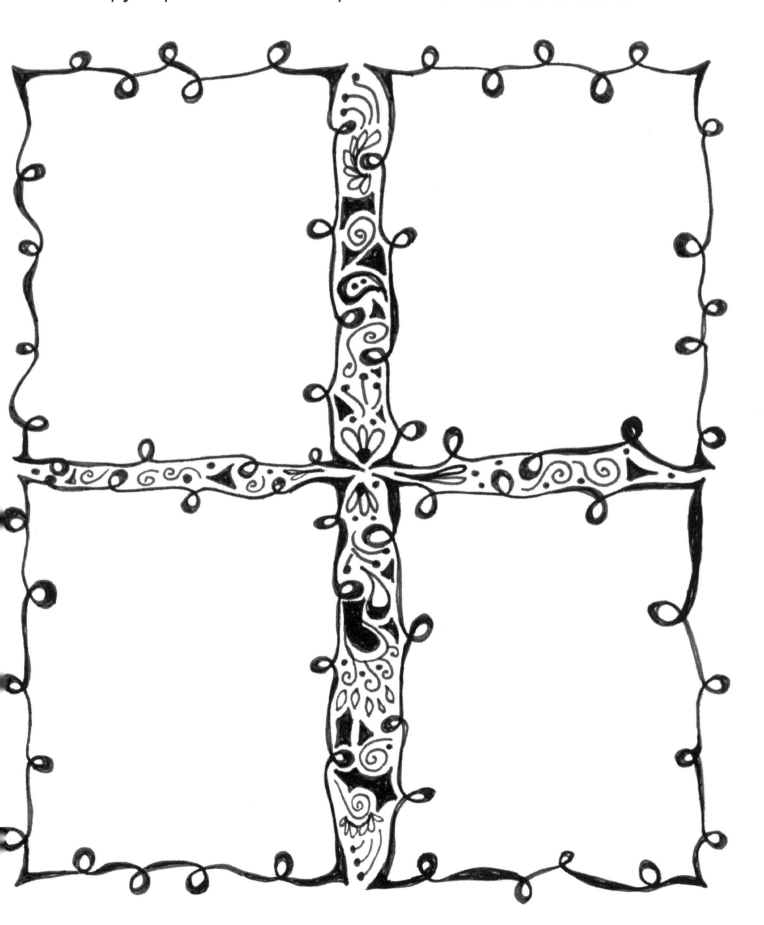

Spelling Time

Find 20 Words with 7 letters each.
Look in your books for words.
Write the words here:

_____   _____

_____   _____

_____   _____

_____   _____

_____   _____

_____   _____

_____   _____

_____   _____

_____   _____

_____   _____

Screen Time!

Watch a Documentary, Educational Program, Movie, or Tutorial.

Start Time: _ _ _ _ _

Stop Time: _ _ _ _ _

TITLE: _____

SUBJECT _____

LOCATION: _____

MESSAGE: _____

_____

Rating:
AWFUL
BAD
LAME
YUCKY
OKAY
NICE
GOOD
GREAT
SUPER
AMAZING

Notes:

TITLE:

Draw a Scene from the video:

Use THIS PAGE for Math Practice

Or be creative and design something, like a house! You could make graphs, maps or geometric designs with this graph paper.

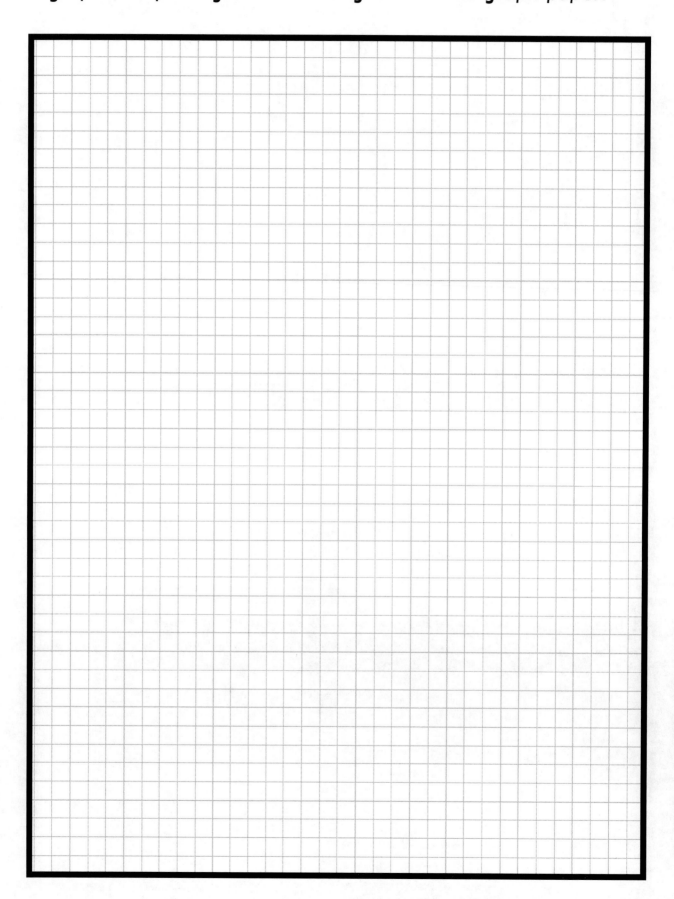

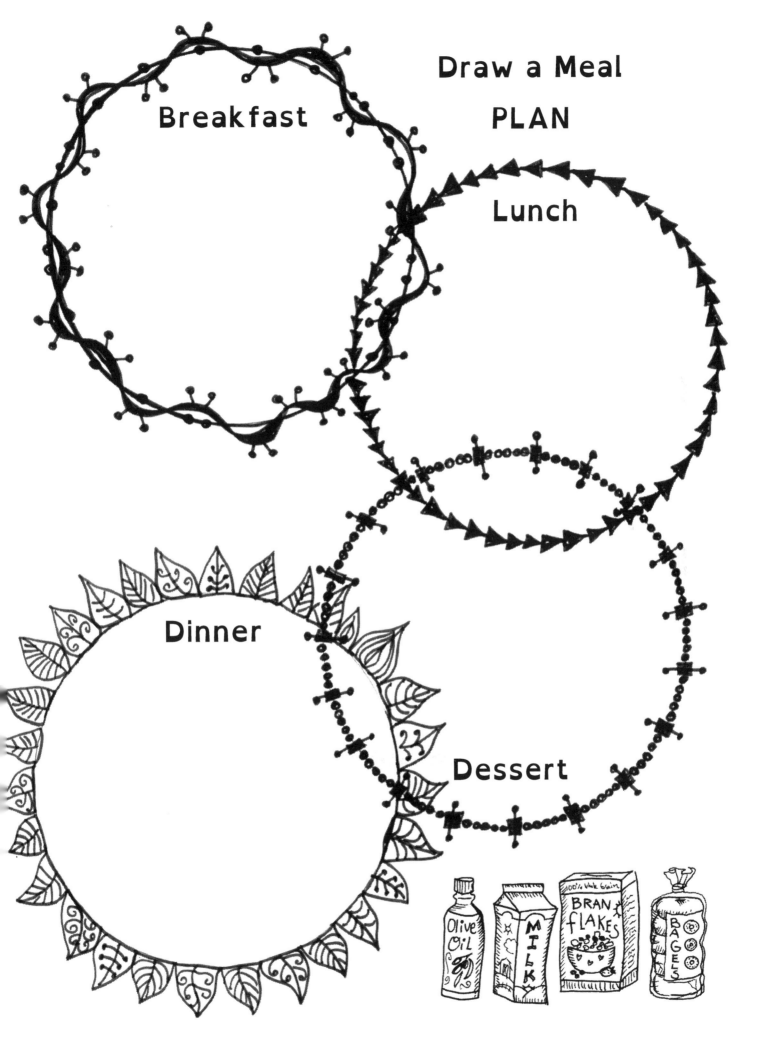

Creative Writing & Copywork

Stories, Poems, Lists and More.

That's what this page is waiting for!

Draw Anything!

Circle Today's Date

January
February
March
April
May
June
July
August
September
October
November
December

1 2 3 4 5 6
7 8 9 10 11
12 13 14 15
16 17 18 19
20 21 22 23
24 25 26 27
28 29 30 31

MONDAY
TUESDAY
WEDNESDAY
THURSDAY
FRIDAY
SATURDAY
SUNDAY

2015
2016
2017
2018
2019
2020
2021
2022
2023
2024
2025
2026
2027
2028
2029

Write Today's Date:_ _ _ _ _ _ _ _ _ _ _ _ _

Start Your Day!

Draw Your Dreams:

To-Do List

_____
_____
_____
_____
_____
_____
_____

Picture Study

Look closely at this picture.

Think about the lines and shadows.

Practice working with your colored pencils.

Draw the Missing Spot

Use a variety of smooth black drawing pens,
with fine points, to complete the picture.

Nature Study

Go outside and make a realistic
drawing of something
you find in nature.

Reading Time - 1 Hour (Set a Timer)

Choose Four Books - Read from each book for 15 minutes.

Copy important words or pictures from each book here:

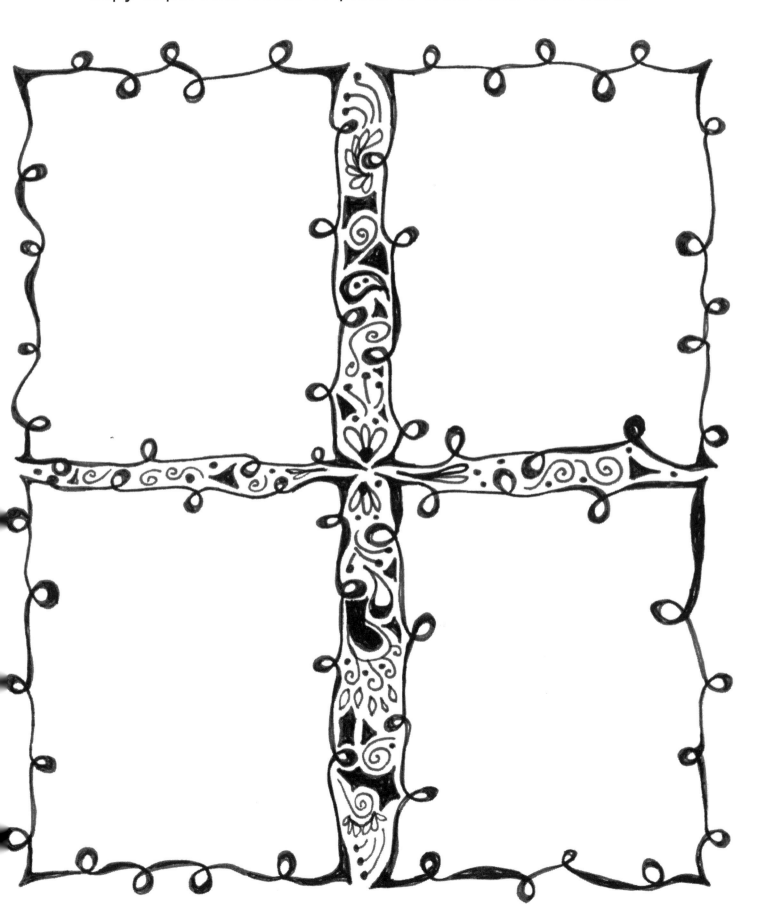

Spelling Time

Find 20 Words with 6 letters each.
Look in your books for words.
Write the words here:

Screen Time!

Watch a Documentary, Educational Program, Movie, or Tutorial.

Start Time: _ _ _ _ _

Stop Time: _ _ _ _ _

TITLE: _____

SUBJECT _____

LOCATION: _____

MESSAGE: _____

_____

Rating:

AWFUL

BAD

LAME

YUCKY

OKAY

NICE

GOOD

GREAT

SUPER

AMAZING

Draw a Scene from the video:

Notes:

TITLE:

Use THIS PAGE for Math Practice

Or be creative and design something, like a house! You could make graphs, maps or geometric designs with this graph paper.

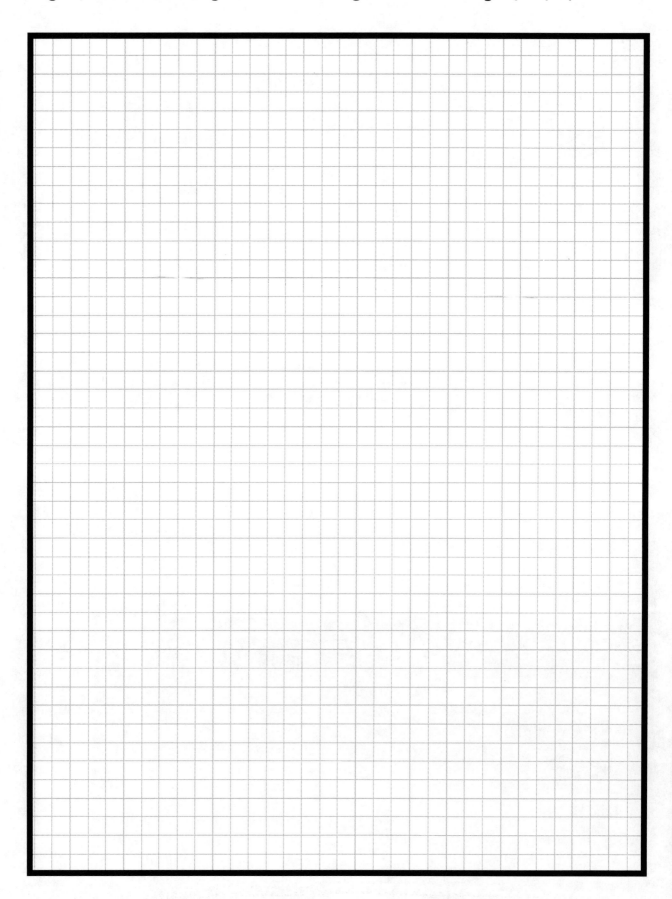

Creative Writing & Copywork

Stories, Poems, Lists and More.
That's what this page is waiting for!

_____

_____

_____

_____

_____

_____

_____

_____

_____

_____

_____

_____

_____

_____

_____

_____

_____

_____

Draw Anything!

Circle Today's Date

January
February
March
April
May
June
July
August
September
October
November
December

1 2 3 4 5 6
7 8 9 10 11
12 13 14 15
16 17 18 19
20 21 22 23
24 25 26 27
28 29 30 31

MONDAY
TUESDAY
WEDNESDAY
THURSDAY
FRIDAY
SATURDAY
SUNDAY

2015
2016
2017
2018
2019
2020
2021
2022
2023
2024
2025
2026
2027
2028
2029

Write Today's Date:_ _ _ _ _ _ _ _ _ _ _ _ _ _ _ _

Start Your Day!

Draw Your Dreams:

To-Do List

_____
_____
_____
_____
_____
_____
_____

Picture Study

Look closely at this picture.

Think about the lines and shadows.

Practice working with your colored pencils.

Draw the Missing Spot

Use a variety of smooth black drawing pens,
with fine points, to complete the picture.

Nature Study

Go outside and make a realistic
drawing of something
you find in nature.

Reading Time - 1 Hour (Set a Timer)

Choose Four Books - Read from each book for 15 minutes.

Copy important words or pictures from each book here:

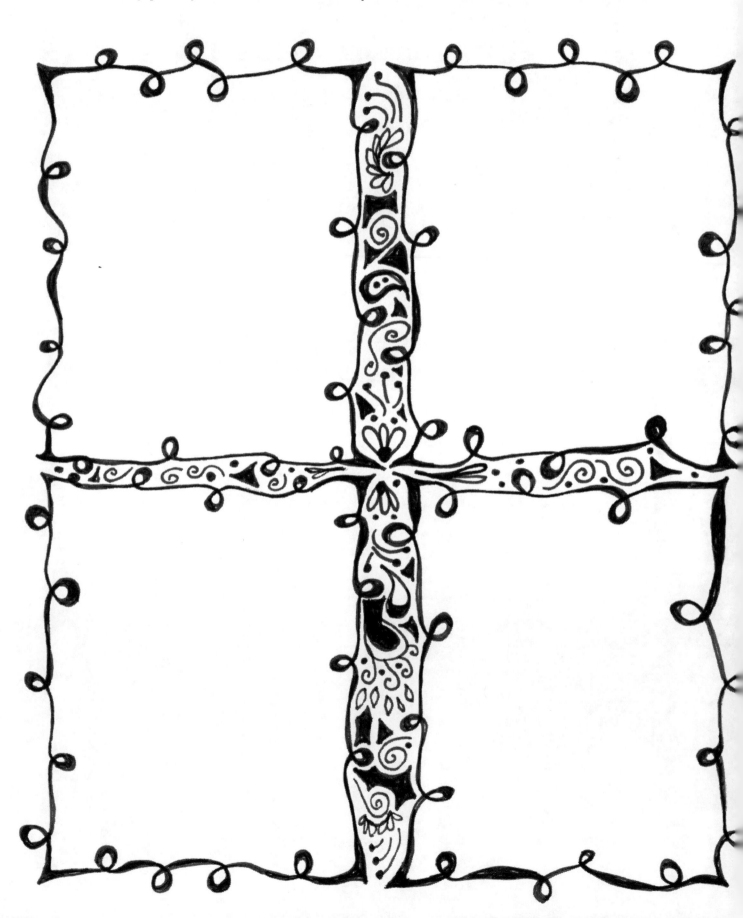

Spelling Time

Find 20 Words with 5 letters each.

Look in your books for words.

Write the words here:

_____   _____

_____   _____

_____   _____

_____   _____

_____   _____

_____   _____

_____   _____

_____   _____

_____   _____

Screen Time!

Watch a Documentary, Educational Program, Movie, or Tutorial.

Start Time:

Stop Time:

TITLE: _____

SUBJECT_____

LOCATION:_____

MESSAGE: _____

_____

Rating:

AWFUL

BAD

LAME

YUCKY

OKAY

NICE

GOOD

GREAT

SUPER

AMAZING

Draw a Scene from the video:

Notes:

TITLE:

Use THIS PAGE for Math Practice

Or be creative and design something, like a house! You could make graphs, maps or geometric designs with this graph paper.

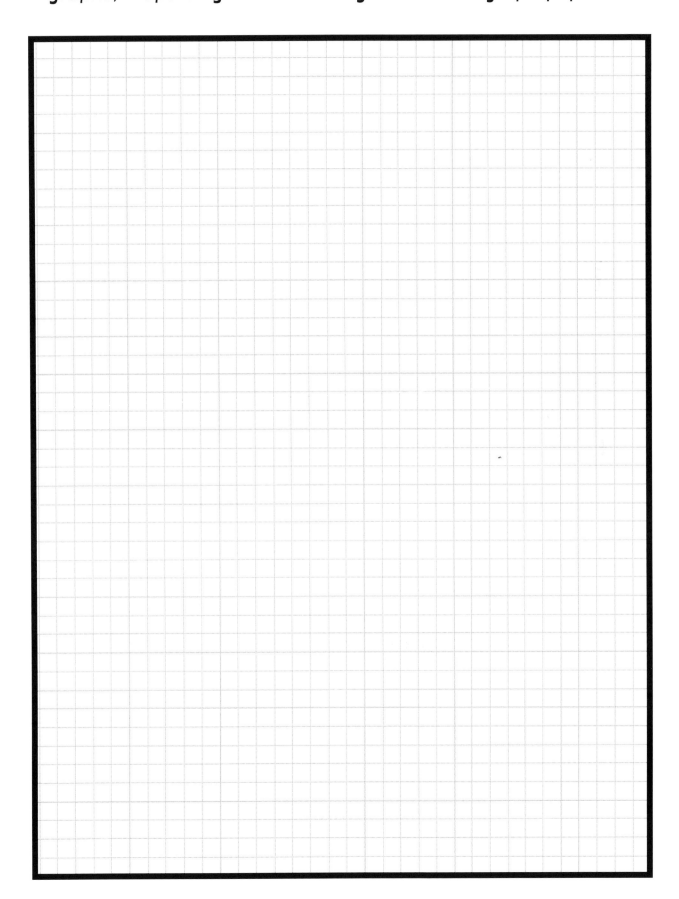

World News Today!

Talk to your parents about current events.

Look at a newspaper, news broadcast or website.

Color the countries you learn about.

Tell the news stories with words or pictures.

Creative Writing & Copywork

Stories, Poems, Lists and More.

That's what this page is waiting for!

_____

_____

_____

_____

_____

_____

_____

_____

_____

_____

_____

_____

_____

_____

_____

_____

My FUN Page

Circle Today's Date

January
February
March
April
May
June
July
August
September
October
November
December

1 2 3 4 5 6
7 8 9 10 11
12 13 14 15
16 17 18 19
20 21 22 23
24 25 26 27
28 29 30 31

MONDAY
TUESDAY
WEDNESDAY
THURSDAY
FRIDAY
SATURDAY
SUNDAY

2015
2016
2017
2018
2019
2020
2021
2022
2023
2024
2025
2026
2027
2028
2029

Write Today's Date:_____

Start Your Day!

Draw Your Dreams:

To-Do List

_____
_____
_____
_____
_____
_____
_____

Picture Study

Look closely at this picture.

Think about the lines and shadows.

Practice working with your colored pencils.

Draw the Missing Spot

Use a variety of smooth black drawing pens,
with fine points, to complete the picture.

Nature Study

Go outside and make a realistic
drawing of something
you find in nature.

Reading Time - 1 Hour (Set a Timer)

Choose Four Books - Read from each book for 15 minutes.

Copy important words or pictures from each book here:

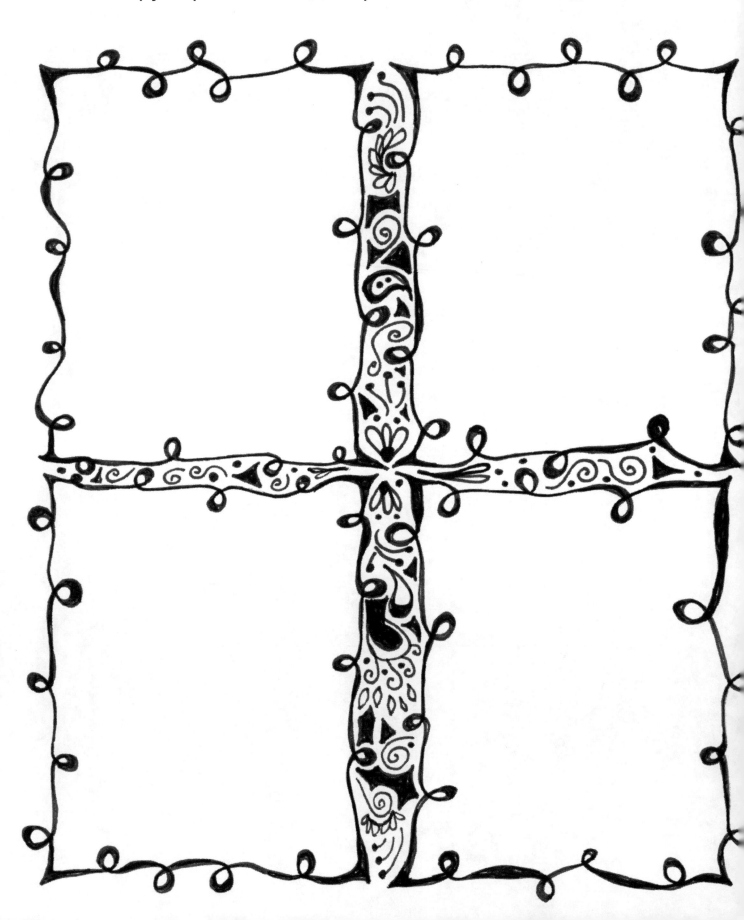

Spelling Time

Find 20 Words with 5 letters each.

Look in your books for words.

Write the words here:

_____   _____

_____   _____

_____   _____

_____   _____

_____   _____

_____   _____

_____   _____

_____   _____

_____   _____

Start Time:

Stop Time:

Screen Time!

Watch a Documentary, Educational Program, Movie, or Tutorial.

TITLE: _____

SUBJECT_____

LOCATION:_____

MESSAGE: _____

_____

Rating:

AWFUL

BAD

LAME

YUCKY

OKAY

NICE

GOOD

GREAT

SUPER

AMAZING

Draw a Scene from the video:

Notes:

TITLE:

Use THIS PAGE for Math Practice

Or be creative and design something, like a house! You could make graphs, maps or geometric designs with this graph paper.

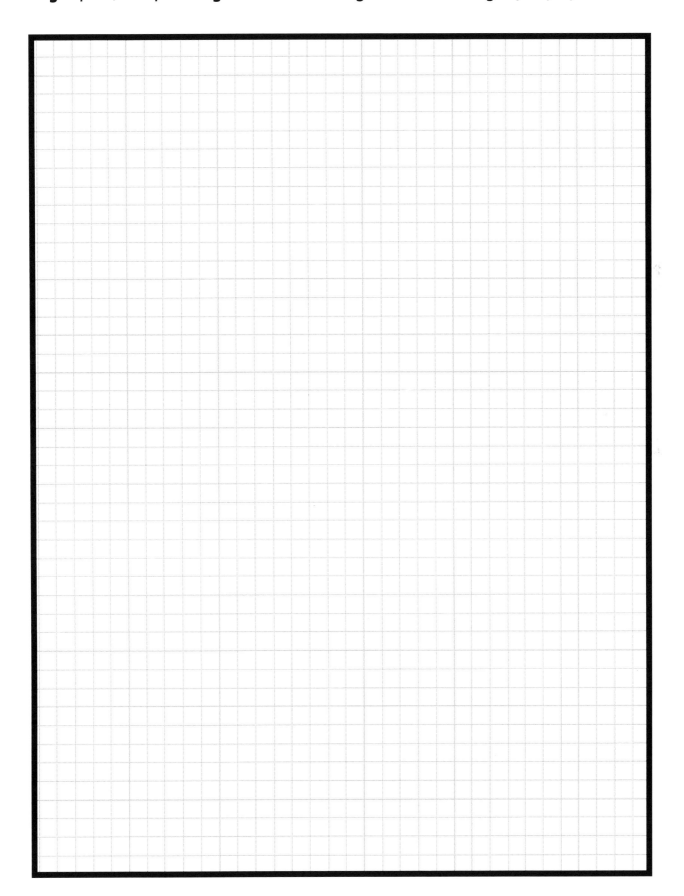

Fun Writing Practice:

ABCDEFGHIJKLMNOPQURSTUVWXYZ

abcdefghijklmnopqrstuvwxyz

ABCDEFGHIJKLMNOPQURSTUVWXYZ

ABCDEFGHIJKLMNOPQURSTUVWXYZ

abcdefghijklmnopqrstuvwxyz

Creative Writing & Copywork

Stories, Poems, Lists and More.

That's what this page is waiting for!

_____

_____

_____

_____

_____

_____

_____

_____

_____

_____

_____

_____

_____

_____

_____

_____

Draw Anything!

Circle Today's Date

January
February
March
April
May
June
July
August
September
October
November
December

1 2 3 4 5 6
7 8 9 10 11
12 13 14 15
16 17 18 19
20 21 22 23
24 25 26 27
28 29 30 31

MONDAY
TUESDAY
WEDNESDAY
THURSDAY
FRIDAY
SATURDAY
SUNDAY

2015
2016
2017
2018
2019
2020
2021
2022
2023
2024
2025
2026
2027
2028
2029

Write Today's Date:_ _ _ _ _ _ _ _ _ _ _ _ _ _ _ _

Start Your Day!

Draw Your Dreams:

To-Do List

_____
_____
_____
_____
_____
_____
_____

Picture Study

Look closely at this picture.

Think about the lines and shadows.

Practice working with your colored pencils.

Draw the Missing Spot

Use a variety of smooth black drawing pens,
with fine points, to complete the picture.

Nature Study

Go outside and make a realistic
drawing of something
you find in nature.

Reading Time - 1 Hour (Set a Timer)

Choose Four Books - Read from each book for 15 minutes.

Copy important words or pictures from each book here:

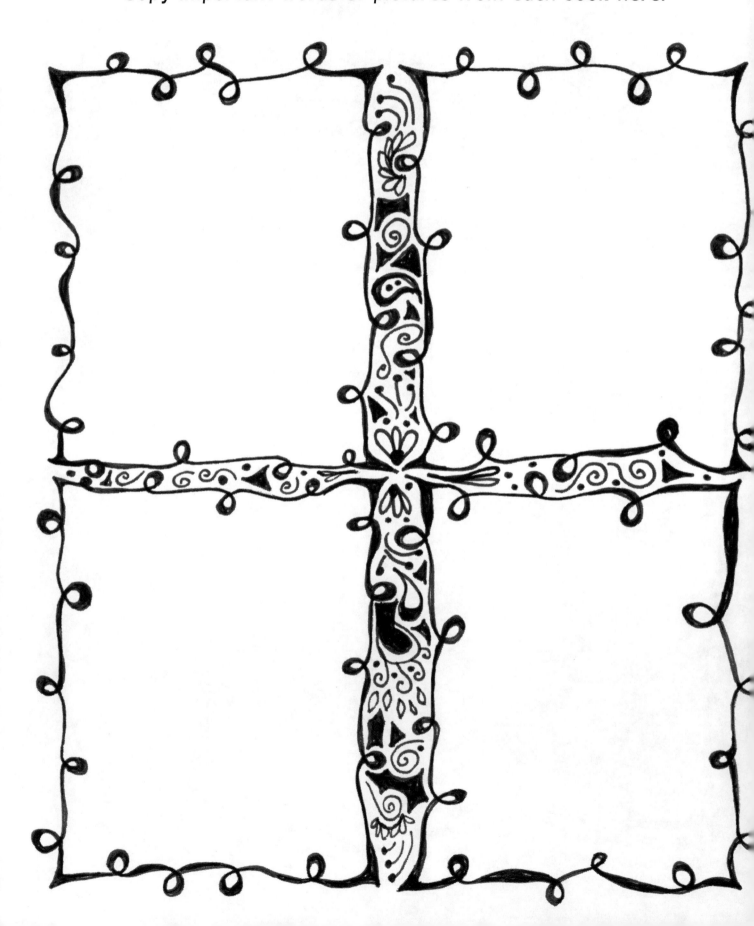

Spelling Time

Find 20 Words with **4** letters each.

Look in your books for words.

Write the words here:

Start Time:

_ _ _ _ _

Stop Time:

_ _ _ _ _

Screen Time!

Watch a Documentary, Educational Program, Movie, or Tutorial.

TITLE: _____

SUBJECT_____

LOCATION:_____

MESSAGE: _____

_____

Rating:

AWFUL

BAD

LAME

YUCKY

OKAY

NICE

GOOD

GREAT

SUPER

AMAZING

Draw a Scene from the video:

Notes:

TITLE:

Use THIS PAGE for Math Practice

Or be creative and design something, like a house! You could make graphs, maps or geometric designs with this graph paper.

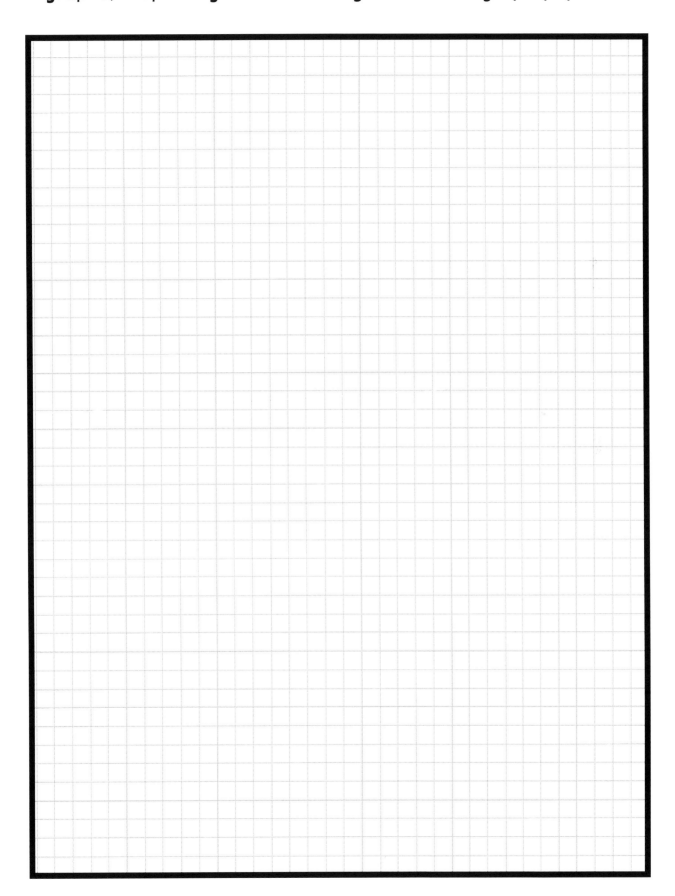

Listening Time

Listen to an audio book or classical music or
ask someone to read a story to you while
you color and draw on the next page.

What are you listening to?

_____

Circle Today's Date

January
February
March
April
May
June
July
August
September
October
November
December

1 2 3 4 5 6
7 8 9 10 11
12 13 14 15
16 17 18 19
20 21 22 23
24 25 26 27
28 29 30 31

MONDAY
TUESDAY
WEDNESDAY
THURSDAY
FRIDAY
SATURDAY
SUNDAY

2015
2016
2017
2018
2019
2020
2021
2022
2023
2024
2025
2026
2027
2028
2029

Write Today's Date:_____

Choose Eight New Books To Use As School Books!

1. Write down the titles on each cover below.
2. Keep your stack of books in a safe place.
3. Be ready to read a few pages from your books daily.
4. Complete 10 pages each day in this workbook.

Start Your Day!

Draw Your Dreams:

To-Do List

_____
_____
_____
_____
_____
_____
_____

Picture Study

Look closely at this picture.

Think about the lines and shadows.

Practice working with your colored pencils.

Draw the Missing Spot

Use a variety of smooth black drawing pens,
with fine points, to complete the picture.

Nature Study

Go outside and make a realistic
drawing of something
you find in nature.

Reading Time - 1 Hour (Set a Timer)

Choose Four Books - Read from each book for 15 minutes.
Copy important words or pictures from each book here:

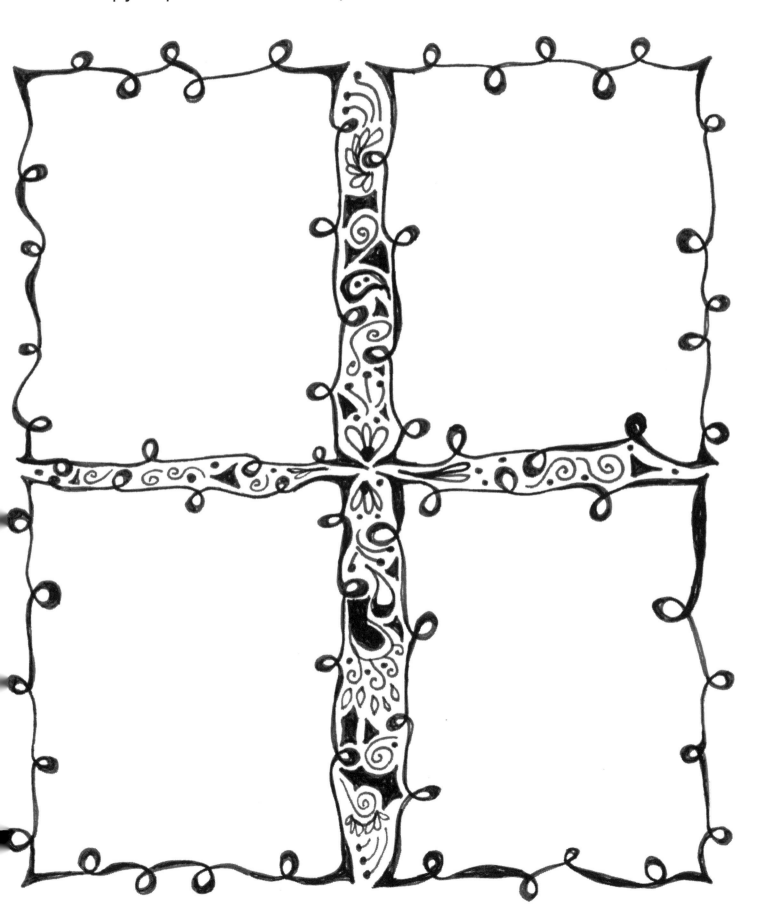

Spelling Time

Find 20 Words with 3 letters each.
Look in your books for words.
Write the words here:

Start Time: _____

Stop Time: _____

Screen Time!

Watch a Documentary, Educational Program, Movie, or Tutorial.

TITLE: _____

SUBJECT _____

LOCATION: _____

MESSAGE: _____

_____

Rating:

AWFUL

BAD

LAME

YUCKY

OKAY

NICE

GOOD

GREAT

SUPER

AMAZING

Draw a Scene from the video:

Notes:

TITLE:

Use THIS PAGE for Math Practice

Or be creative and design something, like a house! You could make graphs, maps or geometric designs with this graph paper.

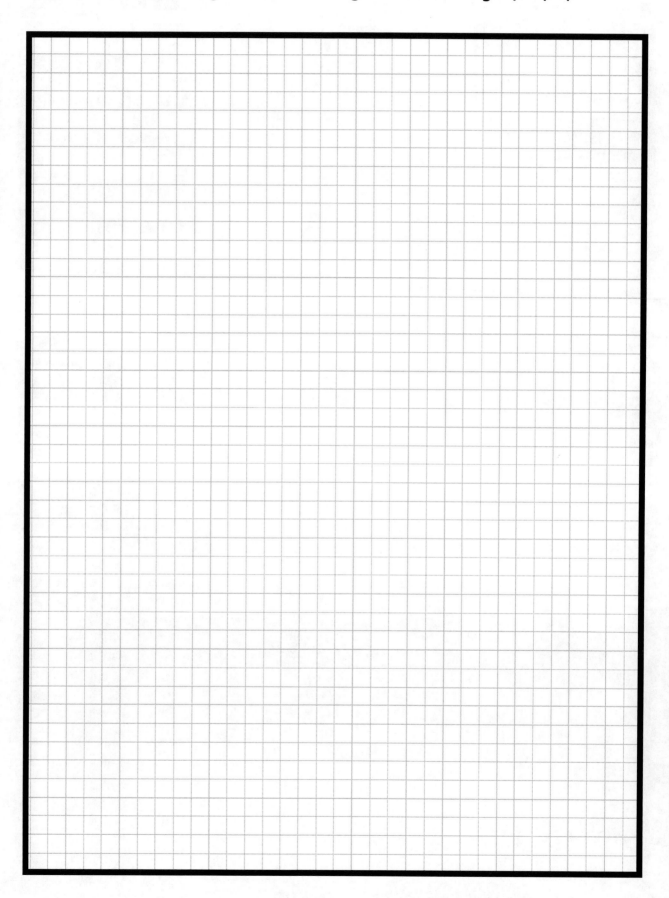

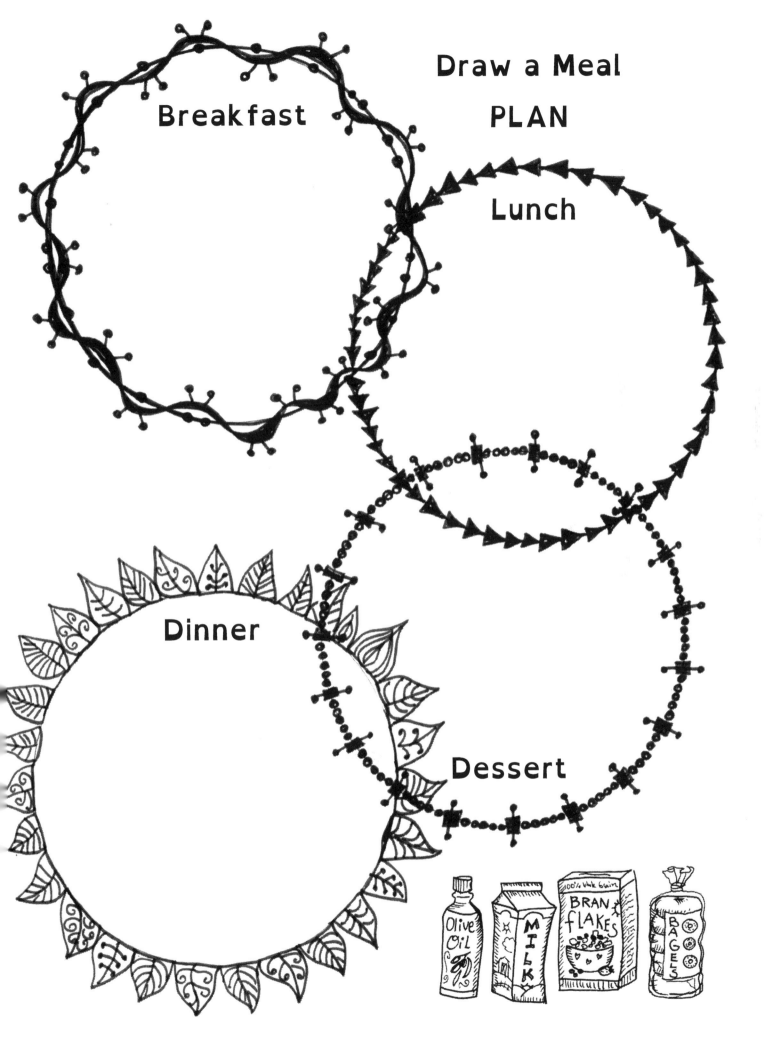

Breakfast

Draw a Meal
PLAN

Lunch

Dinner

Dessert

Creative Writing & Copywork

Stories, Poems, Lists and More.
That's what this page is waiting for!

_____

_____

_____

_____

_____

_____

_____

_____

_____

_____

_____

_____

_____

_____

_____

_____

_____

_____

_____

_____

My FUN Page

Circle Today's Date

January
February
March
April
May
June
July
August
September
October
November
December

1 2 3 4 5 6
7 8 9 10 11
12 13 14 15
16 17 18 19
20 21 22 23
24 25 26 27
28 29 30 31

MONDAY
TUESDAY
WEDNESDAY
THURSDAY
FRIDAY
SATURDAY
SUNDAY

2015
2016
2017
2018
2019
2020
2021
2022
2023
2024
2025
2026
2027
2028
2029

Write Today's Date:_ _ _ _ _ _ _ _ _ _ _ _ _ _ _ _

Start Your Day!

Draw Your Dreams:

To-Do List

_____

_____

_____

_____

_____

_____

Picture Study

Look closely at this picture.

Think about the lines and shadows.

Practice working with your colored pencils.

Draw the Missing Spot

Use a variety of smooth black drawing pens,
with fine points, to complete the picture.

Nature Study

Go outside and make a realistic
drawing of something
you find in nature.

Reading Time - 1 Hour (Set a Timer)

Choose Four Books - Read from each book for 15 minutes.

Copy important words or pictures from each book here:

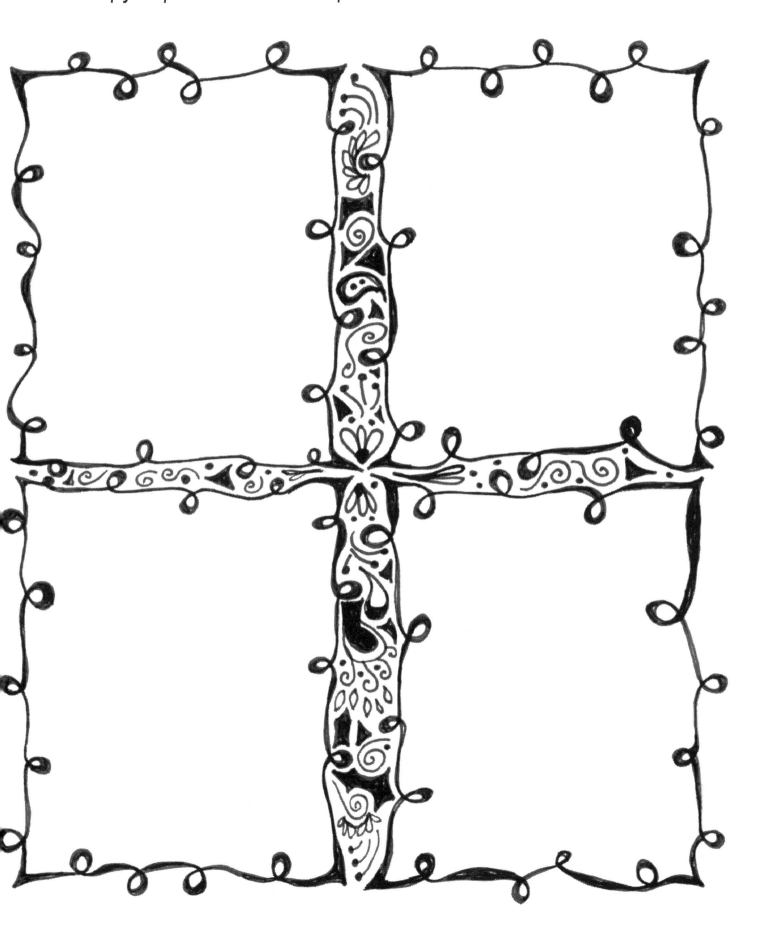

Spelling Time

Find 20 Words with **4** letters each.
Look in your books for words.
Write the words here:

_____   _____

_____   _____

_____   _____

_____   _____

_____   _____

_____   _____

_____   _____

_____   _____

_____   _____

_____   _____

Start Time:

_ _ _ _ _

Stop Time:

_ _ _ _ _

Screen Time!

Watch a Documentary, Educational Program, Movie, or Tutorial.

TITLE: _____

SUBJECT_____

LOCATION:_____

MESSAGE: _____

_____

Rating:

AWFUL

BAD

LAME

YUCKY

OKAY

NICE

GOOD

GREAT

SUPER

AMAZING

Notes:

TITLE:

Draw a Scene from the video:

Use THIS PAGE for Math Practice

Or be creative and design something, like a house! You could make graphs, maps or geometric designs with this graph paper.

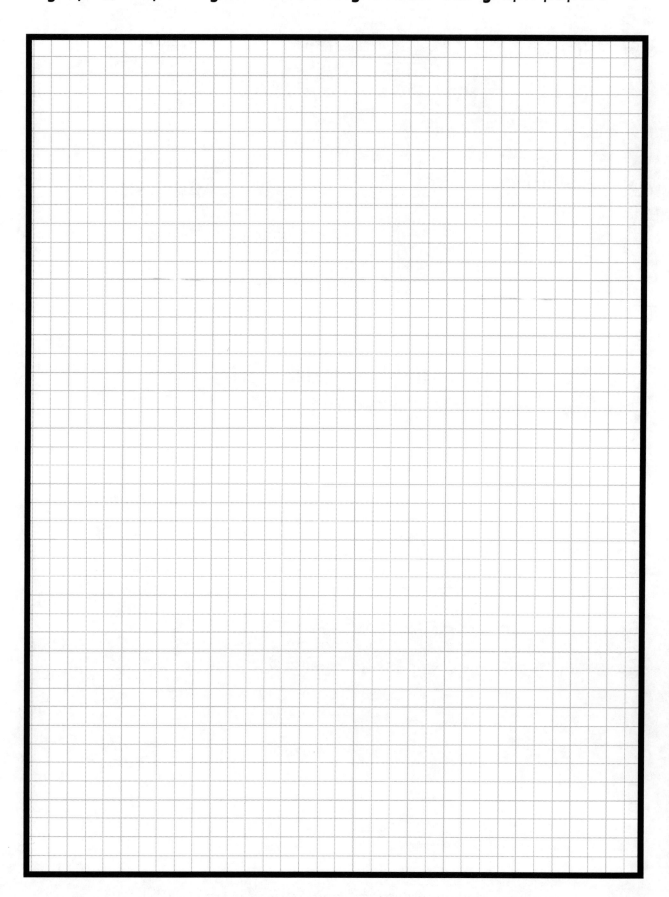

Creative Writing & Copywork

Stories, Poems, Lists and More.
That's what this page is waiting for!

_____

_____

_____

_____

_____

_____

_____

_____

_____

_____

_____

_____

_____

_____

_____

_____

_____

_____

_____

_____

Draw Anything!

Circle Today's Date

January
February
March
April
May
June
July
August
September
October
November
December

1 2 3 4 5 6
7 8 9 10 11
12 13 14 15
16 17 18 19
20 21 22 23
24 25 26 27
28 29 30 31

MONDAY
TUESDAY
WEDNESDAY
THURSDAY
FRIDAY
SATURDAY
SUNDAY

2015
2016
2017
2018
2019
2020
2021
2022
2023
2024
2025
2026
2027
2028
2029

Write Today's Date:_ _ _ _ _ _ _ _ _ _ _ _ _ _ _

Start Your Day!

Draw Your Dreams:

To-Do List

_____
_____
_____
_____
_____
_____
_____

Picture Study

Look closely at this picture.

Think about the lines and shadows.

Practice working with your colored pencils.

Draw the Missing Spot

Use a variety of smooth black drawing pens,
with fine points, to complete the picture.

Nature Study

Go outside and make a realistic
drawing of something
you find in nature.

Reading Time - 1 Hour (Set a Timer)

Choose Four Books - Read from each book for 15 minutes.

Copy important words or pictures from each book here:

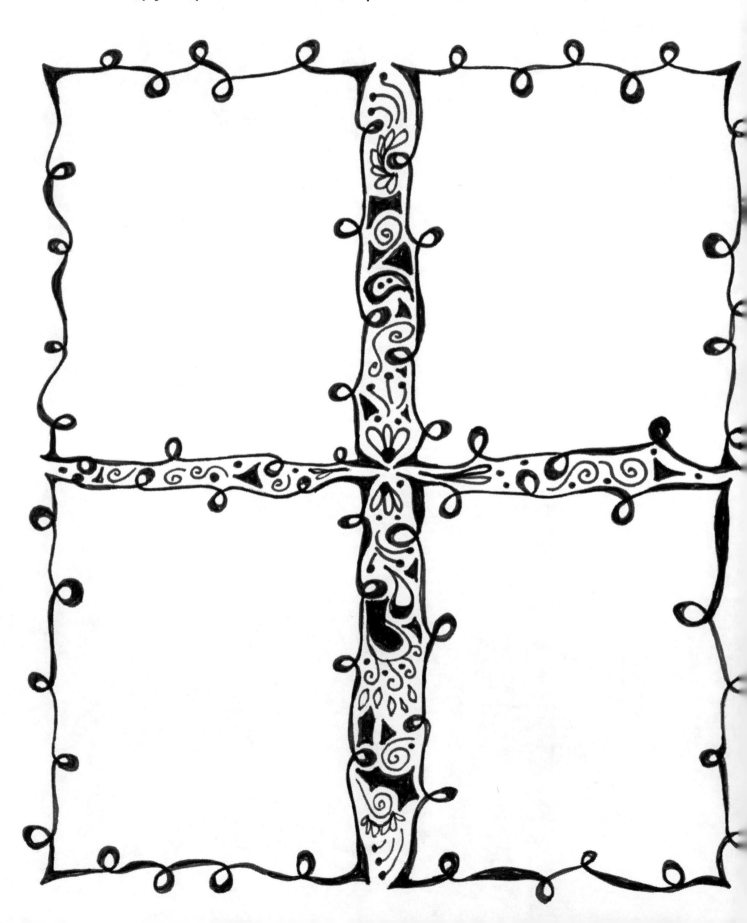

Spelling Time

Find 20 Words with 5 letters each.

Look in your books for words.

Write the words here:

_____   _____

_____   _____

_____   _____

_____   _____

_____   _____

_____   _____

_____   _____

_____   _____

_____   _____

_____   _____

Start Time:
_ _ _ _ _

Stop Time:
_ _ _ _ _

Screen Time!

Watch a Documentary, Educational Program, Movie, or Tutorial.

TITLE: _____

SUBJECT _____

LOCATION: _____

MESSAGE: _____

_____

Rating:
AWFUL
BAD
LAME
YUCKY
OKAY
NICE
GOOD
GREAT
SUPER
AMAZING

Draw a Scene from the video:

Notes:

TITLE:

Use THIS PAGE for Math Practice
Or be creative and design something, like a house! You could make graphs, maps or geometric designs with this graph paper.

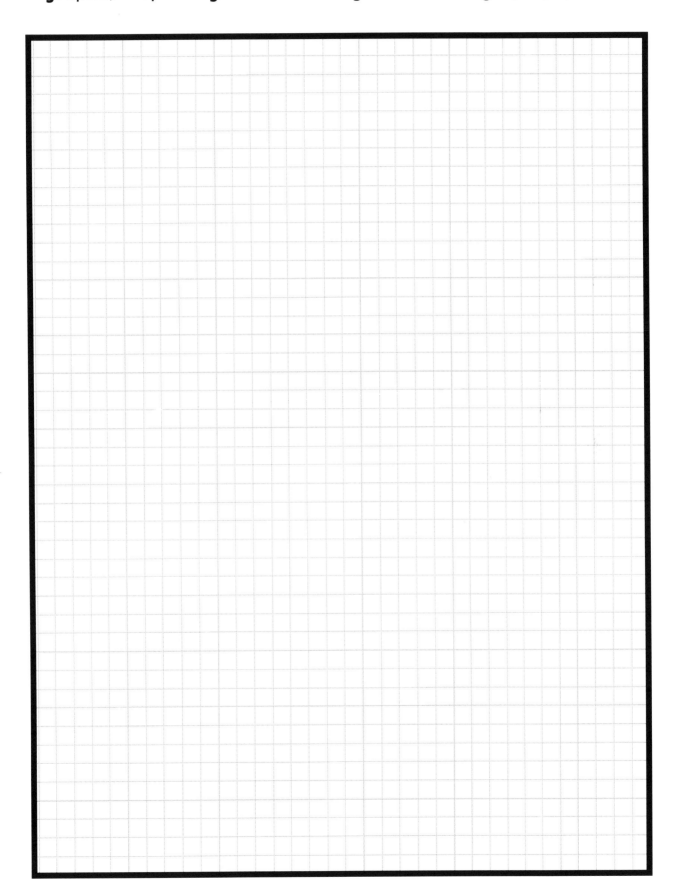

Fun Writing Practice:

ABCDEFGHIJKLMNOPQURSTUVWXYZ

abcdefghijklmnopqrstuvwxyz

ABCDEFGHIJKLMNOPQURSTUVWXYZ

ABCDEFGHIJKLMNOPQURSTUVWXYZ

abcdefghijklmnopqrstuvwxyz

Creative Writing & Copywork

Stories, Poems, Lists and More.

That's what this page is waiting for!

_____

_____

_____

_____

_____

_____

_____

_____

_____

_____

_____

_____

_____

_____

_____

_____

_____

_____

_____

_____

_____

Circle Today's Date

January
February
March
April
May
June
July
August
September
October
November
December

1 2 3 4 5 6
7 8 9 10 11
12 13 14 15
16 17 18 19
20 21 22 23
24 25 26 27
28 29 30 31

MONDAY
TUESDAY
WEDNESDAY
THURSDAY
FRIDAY
SATURDAY
SUNDAY

2015
2016
2017
2018
2019
2020
2021
2022
2023
2024
2025
2026
2027
2028
2029

Write Today's Date: _ _ _ _ _ _ _ _ _ _ _ _ _ _ _ _

Start Your Day!

Draw Your Dreams:

To-Do List

_____
_____
_____
_____
_____
_____
_____

Picture Study

Look closely at this picture.

Think about the lines and shadows.

Practice working with your colored pencils.

Picture Study

Look closely at this picture.

Think about the lines and shadows.

Practice working with your colored pencils.

Nature Study

Go outside and make a realistic
drawing of something
you find in nature.

Reading Time - 1 Hour (Set a Timer)

Choose Four Books - Read from each book for 15 minutes.

Copy important words or pictures from each book here:

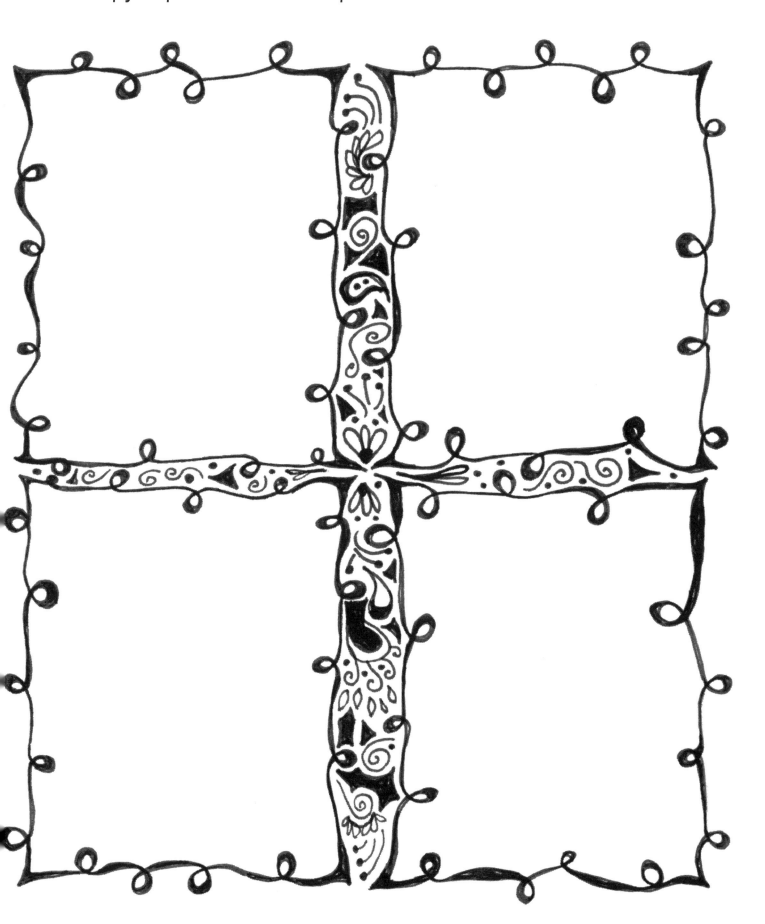

Spelling Time

Find 20 Words with 6 letters each.
Look in your books for words.
Write the words here:

Start Time:

_____

Stop Time:

_____

Screen Time!

Watch a Documentary, Educational Program, Movie, or Tutorial.

TITLE: _____

SUBJECT _____

LOCATION: _____

MESSAGE: _____

_____

Rating:

AWFUL

BAD

LAME

YUCKY

OKAY

NICE

GOOD

GREAT

SUPER

AMAZING

Draw a Scene from the video:

Notes:

TITLE:

Use THIS PAGE for Math Practice

Or be creative and design something, like a house! You could make graphs, maps or geometric designs with this graph paper.

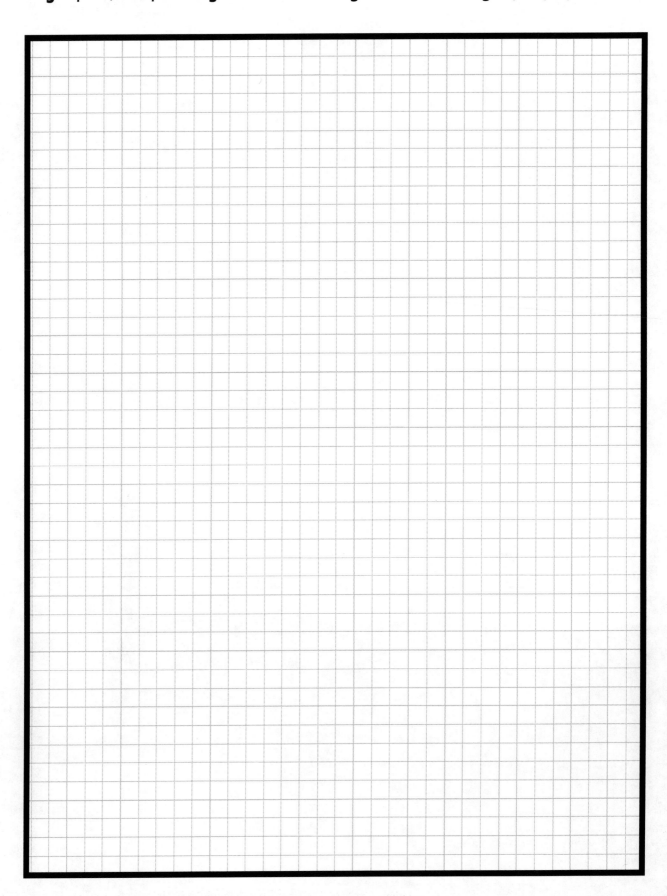

World News Today!

Talk to your parents about current events.

Look at a newspaper, news broadcast or website.

Color the countries you learn about.

Tell the news stories with words or pictures.

Creative Writing & Copywork

Stories, Poems, Lists and More.

That's what this page is waiting for!

Draw Anything!

Circle Today's Date

January
February
March
April
May
June
July
August
September
October
November
December

1 2 3 4 5 6
7 8 9 10 11
12 13 14 15
16 17 18 19
20 21 22 23
24 25 26 27
28 29 30 31

MONDAY
TUESDAY
WEDNESDAY
THURSDAY
FRIDAY
SATURDAY
SUNDAY

2015
2016
2017
2018
2019
2020
2021
2022
2023
2024
2025
2026
2027
2028
2029

Write Today's Date:_ _ _ _ _ _ _ _ _ _ _ _ _ _ _

Start Your Day!

Draw Your Dreams:

To-Do List

_____
_____
_____
_____
_____
_____
_____

Picture Study

Look closely at this picture.

Think about the lines and shadows.

Practice working with your colored pencils.

Draw the Missing Spot

Use a variety of smooth black drawing pens,
with fine points, to complete the picture.

Nature Study

Go outside and make a realistic
drawing of something
you find in nature.

Reading Time - 1 Hour (Set a Timer)

Choose Four Books - Read from each book for 15 minutes.

Copy important words or pictures from each book here:

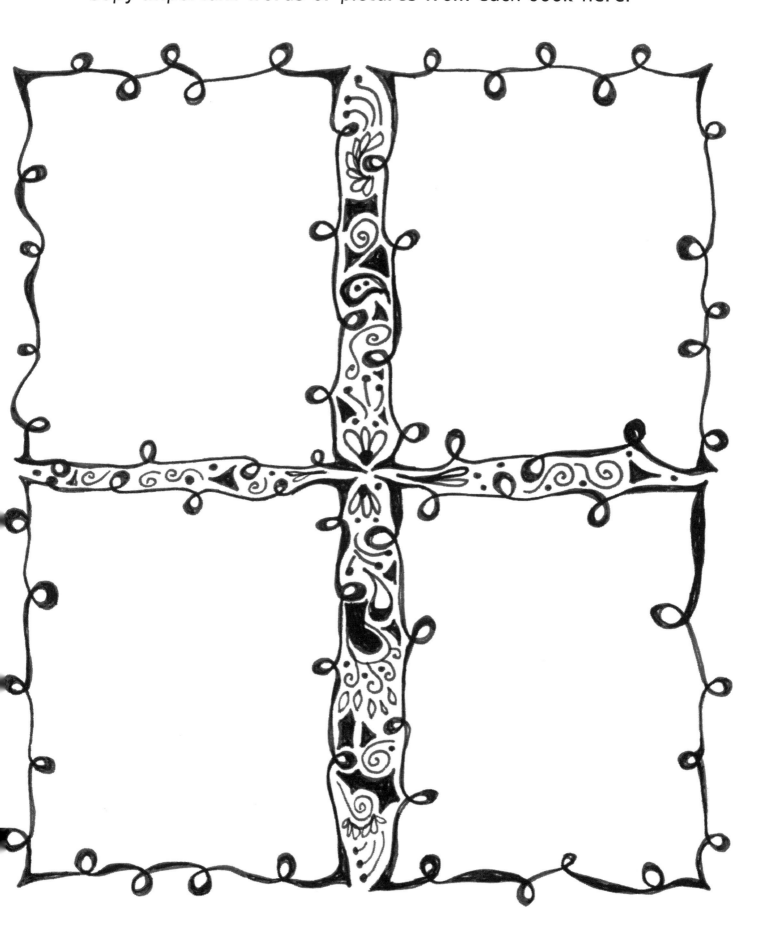

Spelling Time

Find 20 Words with **7** letters each.
Look in your books for words.
Write the words here:

Start Time:

Stop Time:

Screen Time!

Watch a Documentary, Educational Program, Movie, or Tutorial.

TITLE: _____

SUBJECT _____

LOCATION: _____

MESSAGE: _____

_____

Rating:

AWFUL

BAD

LAME

YUCKY

OKAY

NICE

GOOD

GREAT

SUPER

AMAZING

Notes:

TITLE!

Draw a Scene from the video:

Use THIS PAGE for Math Practice

Or be creative and design something, like a house! You could make graphs, maps or geometric designs with this graph paper.

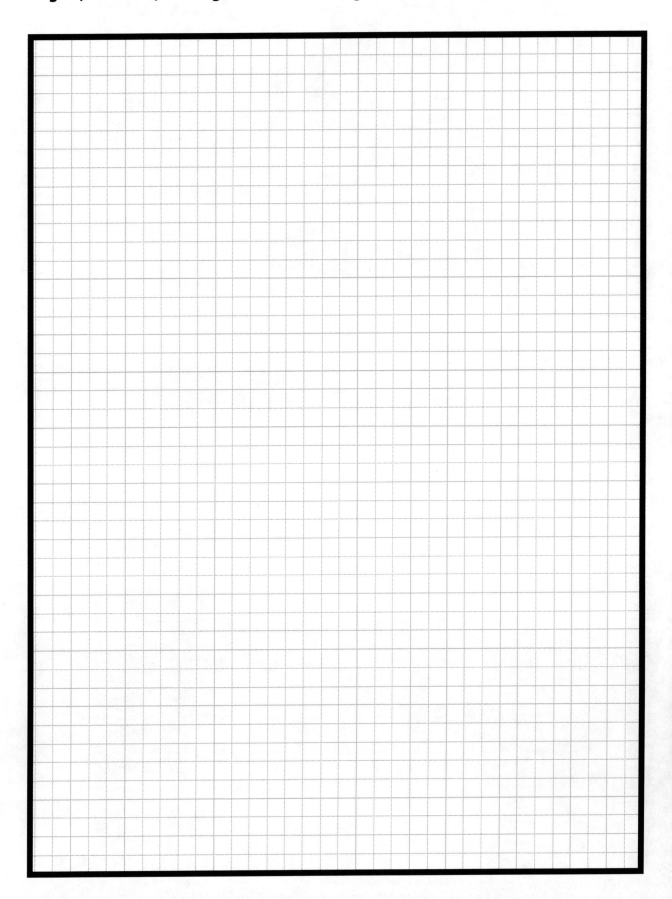

Creative Writing & Copywork

Stories, Poems, Lists and More.

That's what this page is waiting for!

_____

_____

_____

_____

_____

_____

_____

_____

_____

_____

_____

_____

_____

_____

_____

_____

_____

My FUN Page

Circle Today's Date

January
February
March
April
May
June
July
August
September
October
November
December

1 2 3 4 5 6
7 8 9 10 11
12 13 14 15
16 17 18 19
20 21 22 23
24 25 26 27
28 29 30 31

MONDAY
TUESDAY
WEDNESDAY
THURSDAY
FRIDAY
SATURDAY
SUNDAY

2015
2016
2017
2018
2019
2020
2021
2022
2023
2024
2025
2026
2027
2028
2029

Write Today's Date:_____

Start Your Day!

Draw Your Dreams:

To-Do List

_____
_____
_____
_____
_____
_____
_____

Picture Study

Look closely at this picture.

Think about the lines and shadows.

Practice working with your colored pencils.

Draw the Missing Spot

Use a variety of smooth black drawing pens,
with fine points, to complete the picture.

Nature Study

Go outside and make a realistic
drawing of something
you find in nature.

Reading Time - 1 Hour (Set a Timer)

Choose Four Books - Read from each book for 15 minutes.

Copy important words or pictures from each book here:

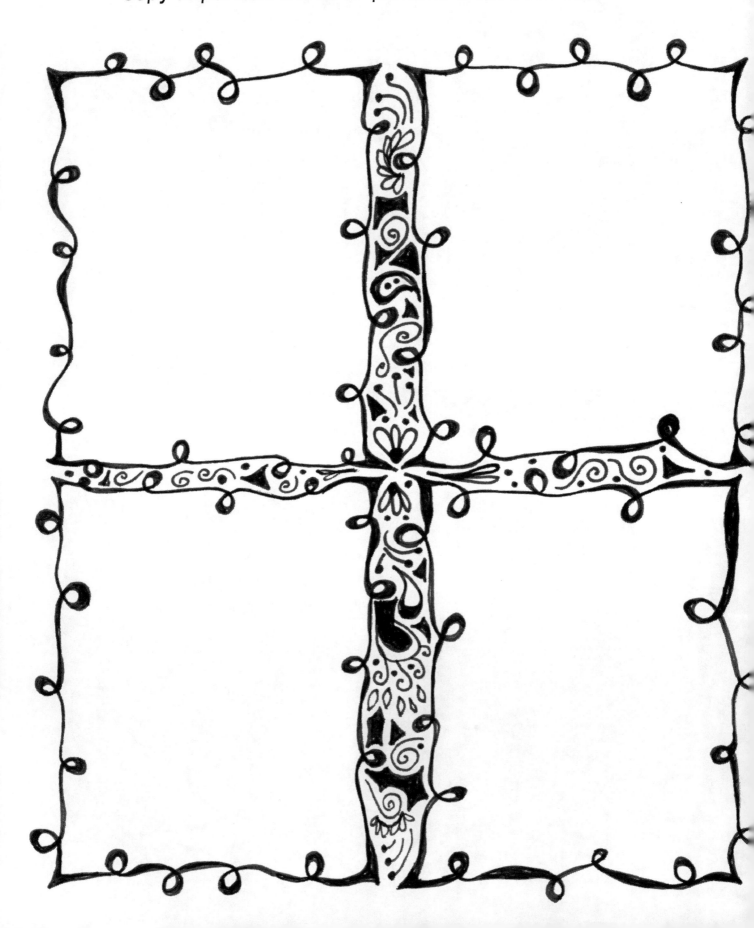

Spelling Time

Find 20 Words with 8 letters each.

Look in your books for words.

Write the words here:

_____   _____

_____   _____

_____   _____

_____   _____

_____   _____

_____   _____

_____   _____

_____   _____

_____   _____

Start Time:

_ _ _ _ _

Stop Time:

_ _ _ _ _

Screen Time!

Watch a Documentary, Educational Program, Movie, or Tutorial.

TITLE: _____

SUBJECT_____

LOCATION:_____

MESSAGE: _____

_____

Rating:

AWFUL

BAD

LAME

YUCKY

OKAY

NICE

GOOD

GREAT

SUPER

AMAZING

Draw a Scene from the video:

Notes:

TITLE:

Use THIS PAGE for Math Practice

Or be creative and design something, like a house! You could make graphs, maps or geometric designs with this graph paper.

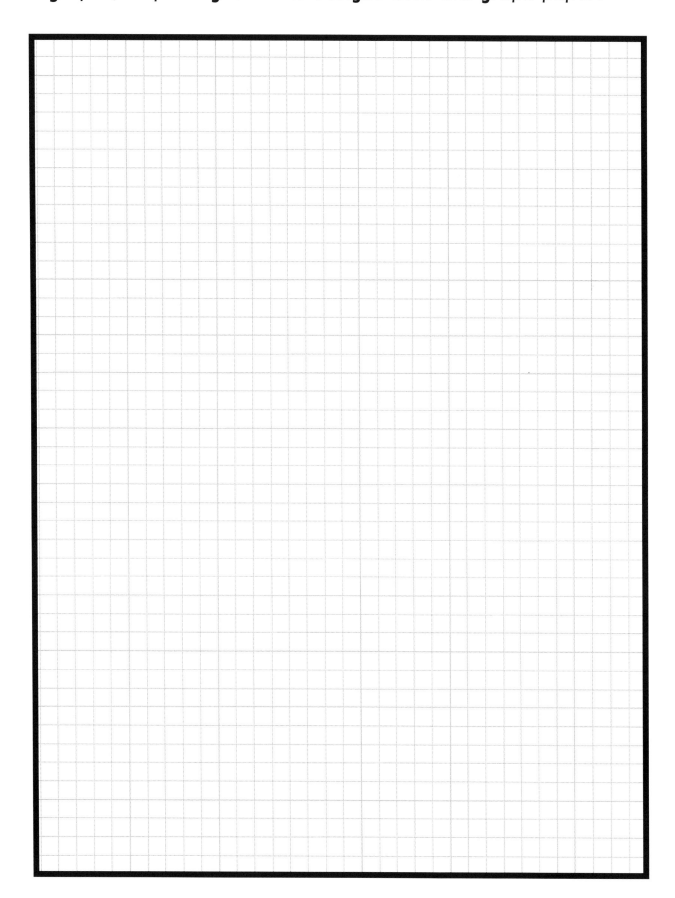

Listening Time

Listen to an audio book or classical music or
ask someone to read a story to you while
you color and draw on the next page.

What are you listening to?

_____

Draw Anything!

Circle Today's Date

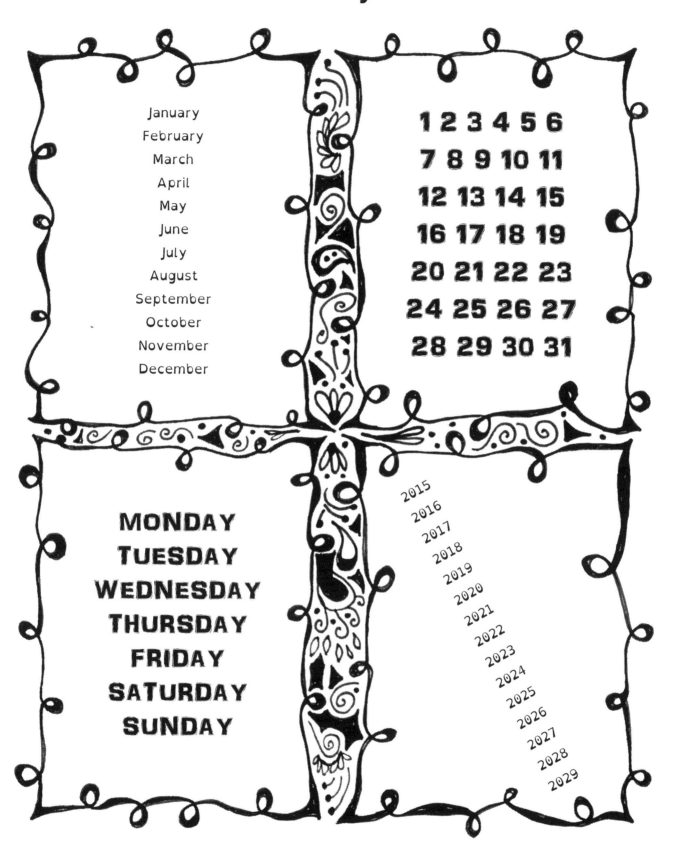

January
February
March
April
May
June
July
August
September
October
November
December

1 2 3 4 5 6
7 8 9 10 11
12 13 14 15
16 17 18 19
20 21 22 23
24 25 26 27
28 29 30 31

MONDAY
TUESDAY
WEDNESDAY
THURSDAY
FRIDAY
SATURDAY
SUNDAY

2015
2016
2017
2018
2019
2020
2021
2022
2023
2024
2025
2026
2027
2028
2029

Write Today's Date: _ _ _ _ _ _ _ _ _ _ _ _ _ _ _ _ _

Start Your Day!

Draw Your Dreams:

To-Do List

_____
_____
_____
_____
_____
_____
_____

Picture Study

Look closely at this picture.

Think about the lines and shadows.

Practice working with your colored pencils.

Draw the Missing Spot

Use a variety of smooth black drawing pens,
with fine points, to complete the picture.

Nature Study

Go outside and make a realistic
drawing of something
you find in nature.

Reading Time - 1 Hour (Set a Timer)

Choose Four Books - Read from each book for 15 minutes.

Copy important words or pictures from each book here:

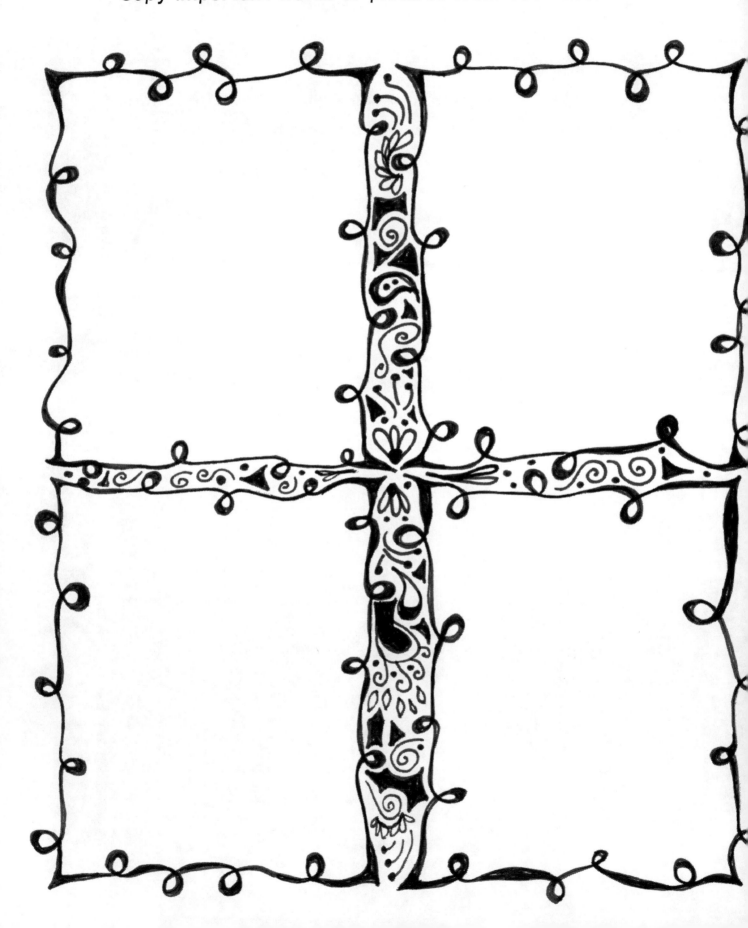

Spelling Time

Find 20 Words with **9** letters each.

Look in your books for words.

Write the words here:

_____   _____

_____   _____

_____   _____

_____   _____

_____   _____

_____   _____

_____   _____

_____   _____

_____   _____

_____   _____

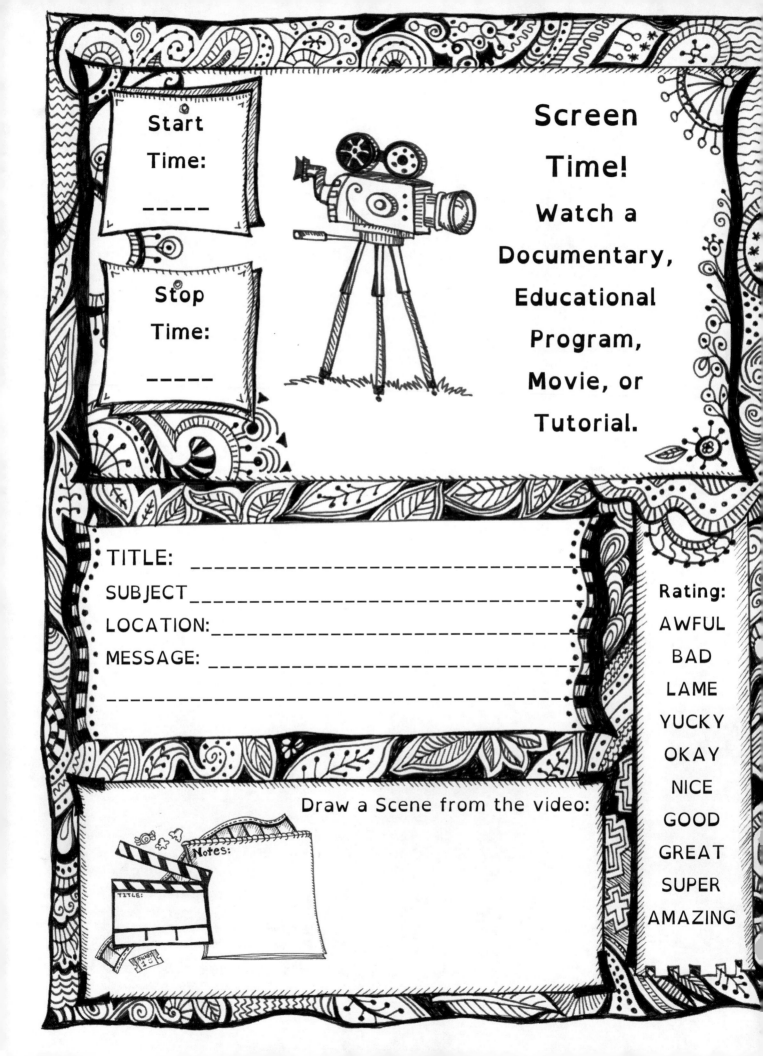

Screen Time!

Watch a Documentary, Educational Program, Movie, or Tutorial.

Start Time: _____

Stop Time: _____

TITLE: _____

SUBJECT_____

LOCATION:_____

MESSAGE: _____

_____

Rating:
AWFUL
BAD
LAME
YUCKY
OKAY
NICE
GOOD
GREAT
SUPER
AMAZING

Draw a Scene from the video:

Notes:

TITLE:

Use THIS PAGE for Math Practice

Or be creative and design something, like a house! You could make graphs, maps or geometric designs with this graph paper.

World News Today!

Talk to your parents about current events.

Look at a newspaper, news broadcast or website.

Color the countries you learn about.

Tell the news stories with words or pictures.

Creative Writing & Copywork

Stories, Poems, Lists and More.

That's what this page is waiting for!

_____

_____

_____

_____

_____

_____

_____

_____

_____

_____

_____

_____

_____

_____

_____

_____

_____

_____

_____

Circle Today's Date

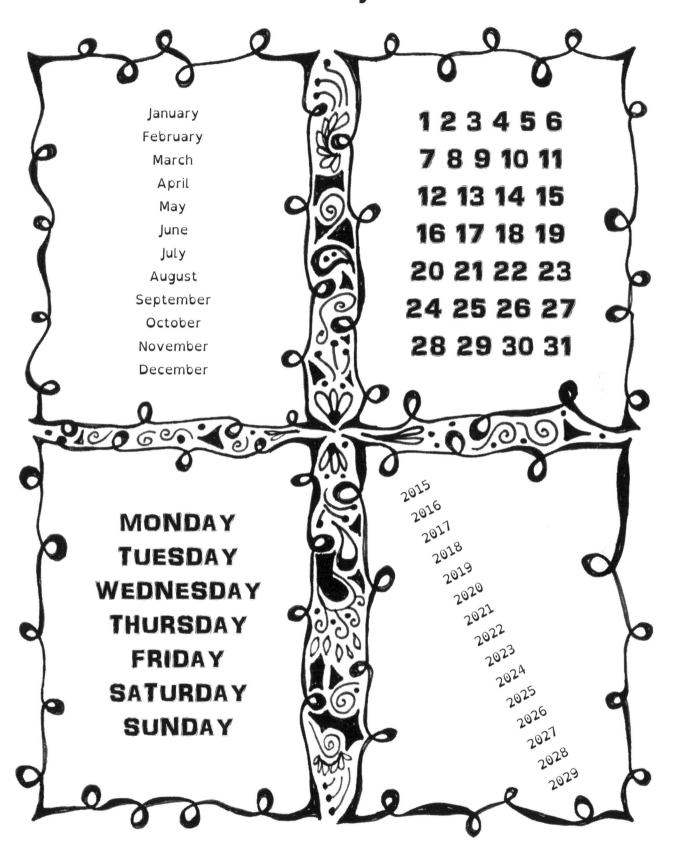

January
February
March
April
May
June
July
August
September
October
November
December

1 2 3 4 5 6
7 8 9 10 11
12 13 14 15
16 17 18 19
20 21 22 23
24 25 26 27
28 29 30 31

MONDAY
TUESDAY
WEDNESDAY
THURSDAY
FRIDAY
SATURDAY
SUNDAY

2015
2016
2017
2018
2019
2020
2021
2022
2023
2024
2025
2026
2027
2028
2029

Write Today's Date: _ _ _ _ _ _ _ _ _ _ _ _ _ _ _ _ _

Start Your Day!

Draw Your Dreams:

To-Do List

_____
_____
_____
_____
_____
_____
_____

Picture Study

Look closely at this picture.
Think about the lines and shadows.
Practice working with your colored pencils.

Draw the Missing Spot

Use a variety of smooth black drawing pens,
with fine points, to complete the picture.

Nature Study

Go outside and make a realistic
drawing of something
you find in nature.

Reading Time - 1 Hour (Set a Timer)

Choose Four Books - Read from each book for 15 minutes.

Copy important words or pictures from each book here:

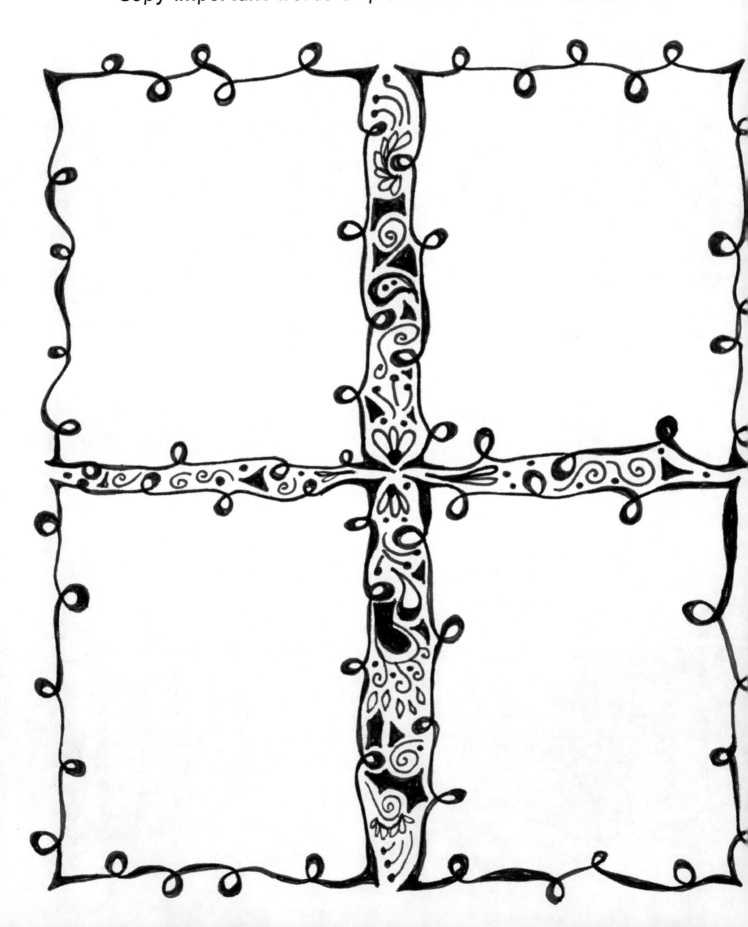

Spelling Time

Find 20 Words with 8 letters each.

Look in your books for words.

Write the words here:

Screen Time!

Watch a Documentary, Educational Program, Movie, or Tutorial.

Start Time:

_____

Stop Time:

_____

TITLE: _____

SUBJECT_____

LOCATION:_____

MESSAGE: _____

_____

Rating:

AWFUL

BAD

LAME

YUCKY

OKAY

NICE

GOOD

GREAT

SUPER

AMAZING

Draw a Scene from the video:

Notes:

TITLE:

Use THIS PAGE for Math Practice

Or be creative and design something, like a house! You could make graphs, maps or geometric designs with this graph paper.

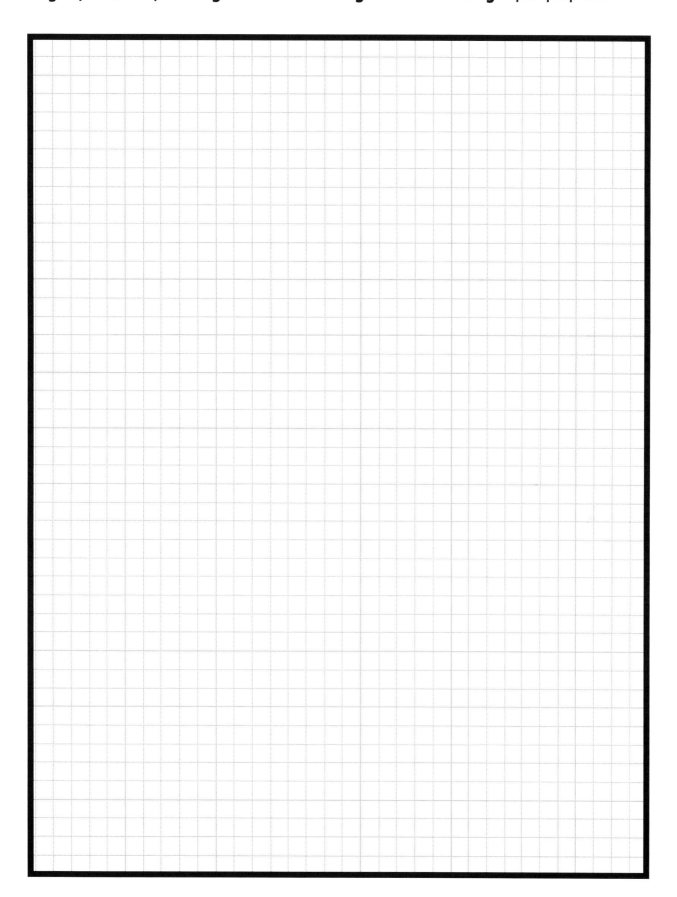

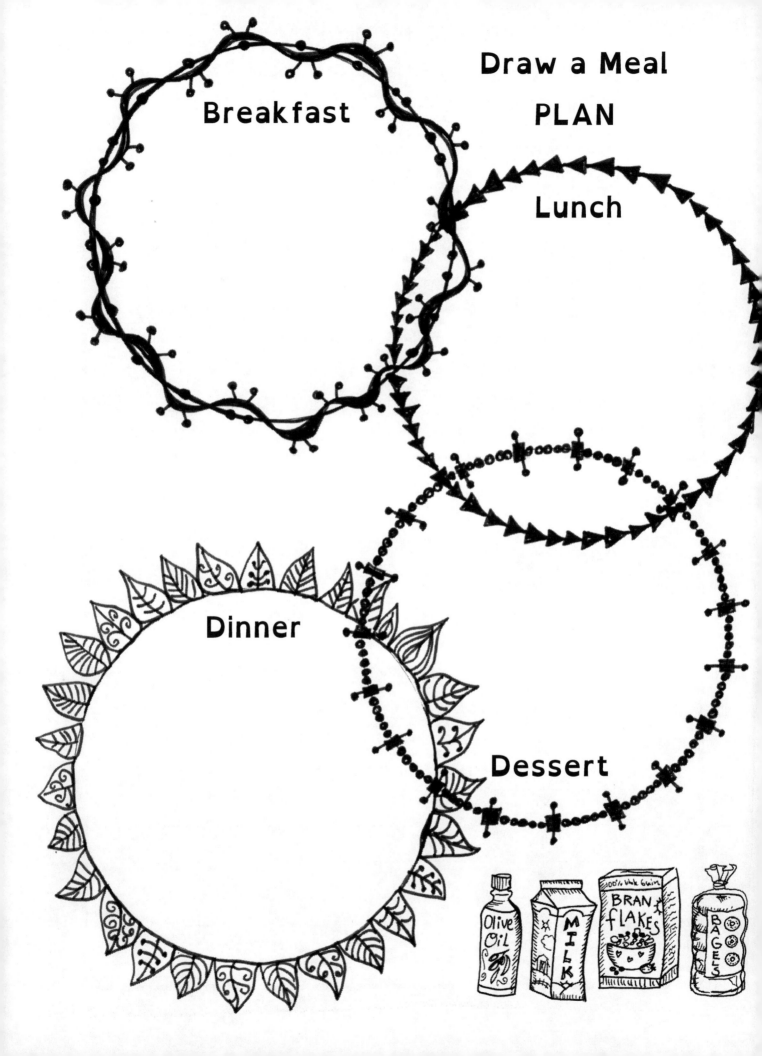

Creative Writing & Copywork

Stories, Poems, Lists and More.

That's what this page is waiting for!

Draw Anything!

Circle Today's Date

January
February
March
April
May
June
July
August
September
October
November
December

1 2 3 4 5 6
7 8 9 10 11
12 13 14 15
16 17 18 19
20 21 22 23
24 25 26 27
28 29 30 31

MONDAY
TUESDAY
WEDNESDAY
THURSDAY
FRIDAY
SATURDAY
SUNDAY

2015
2016
2017
2018
2019
2020
2021
2022
2023
2024
2025
2026
2027
2028
2029

Write Today's Date: _ _ _ _ _ _ _ _ _ _ _ _ _ _ _ _ _

Start Your Day!

Draw Your Dreams:

To-Do List

_____
_____
_____
_____
_____
_____

Picture Study

Look closely at this picture.

Think about the lines and shadows.

Practice working with your colored pencils.

Draw the Missing Spot

Use a variety of smooth black drawing pens,
with fine points, to complete the picture.

Nature Study

Go outside and make a realistic
drawing of something
you find in nature.

Reading Time - 1 Hour (Set a Timer)

Choose Four Books - Read from each book for 15 minutes.

Copy important words or pictures from each book here:

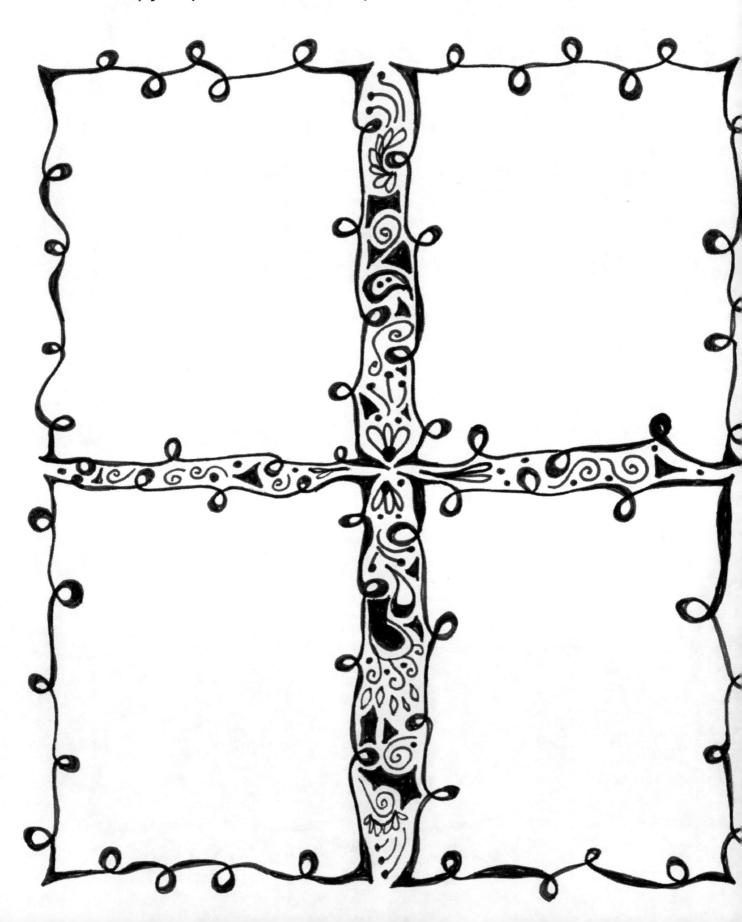

Spelling Time

Find 20 Words with **8** letters each.

Look in your books for words.

Write the words here:

_____   _____

_____   _____

_____   _____

_____   _____

_____   _____

_____   _____

_____   _____

_____   _____

_____   _____

_____   _____

Screen Time!

Watch a Documentary, Educational Program, Movie, or Tutorial.

Start Time: _____

Stop Time: _____

TITLE: _____

SUBJECT _____

LOCATION: _____

MESSAGE: _____

_____

Rating:

AWFUL

BAD

LAME

YUCKY

OKAY

NICE

GOOD

GREAT

SUPER

AMAZING

Draw a Scene from the video:

Notes:

TITLE:

Use THIS PAGE for Math Practice

Or be creative and design something, like a house! You could make graphs, maps or geometric designs with this graph paper.

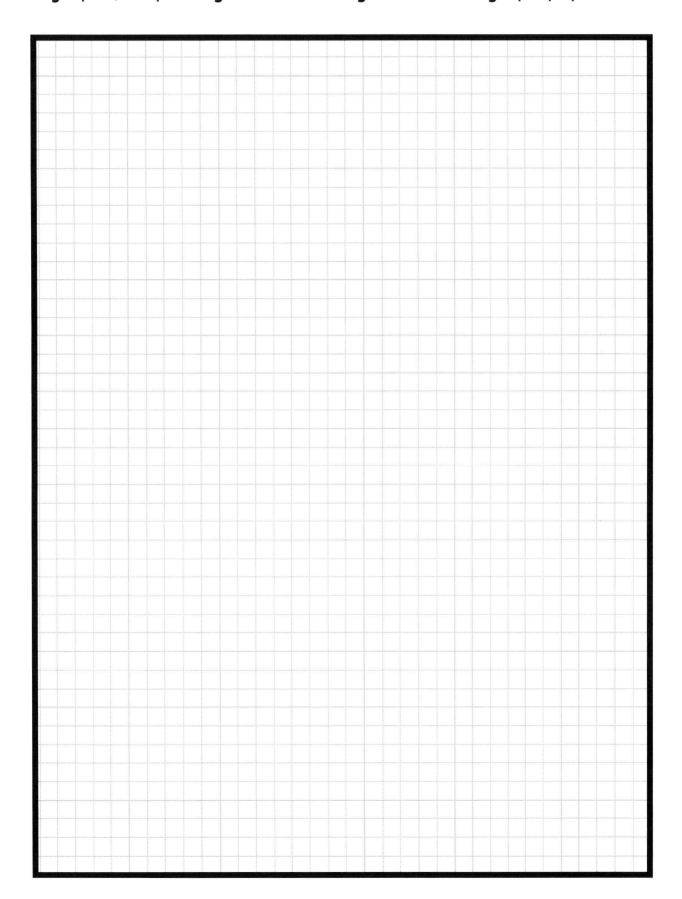

Creative Writing & Copywork

Stories, Poems, Lists and More.

That's what this page is waiting for!

_____

_____

_____

_____

_____

_____

_____

_____

_____

_____

_____

_____

_____

_____

_____

_____

_____

_____

_____

Draw Anything!

My FUN Page

Start Your Day!

Draw Your Dreams:

To-Do List

_____
_____
_____
_____
_____
_____
_____

Picture Study

Look closely at this picture.

Think about the lines and shadows.

Practice working with your colored pencils.

Draw the Missing Spot

Use a variety of smooth black drawing pens,
with fine points, to complete the picture.

Nature Study

Go outside and make a realistic
drawing of something
you find in nature.

Reading Time - 1 Hour (Set a Timer)

Choose Four Books - Read from each book for 15 minutes.

Copy important words or pictures from each book here:

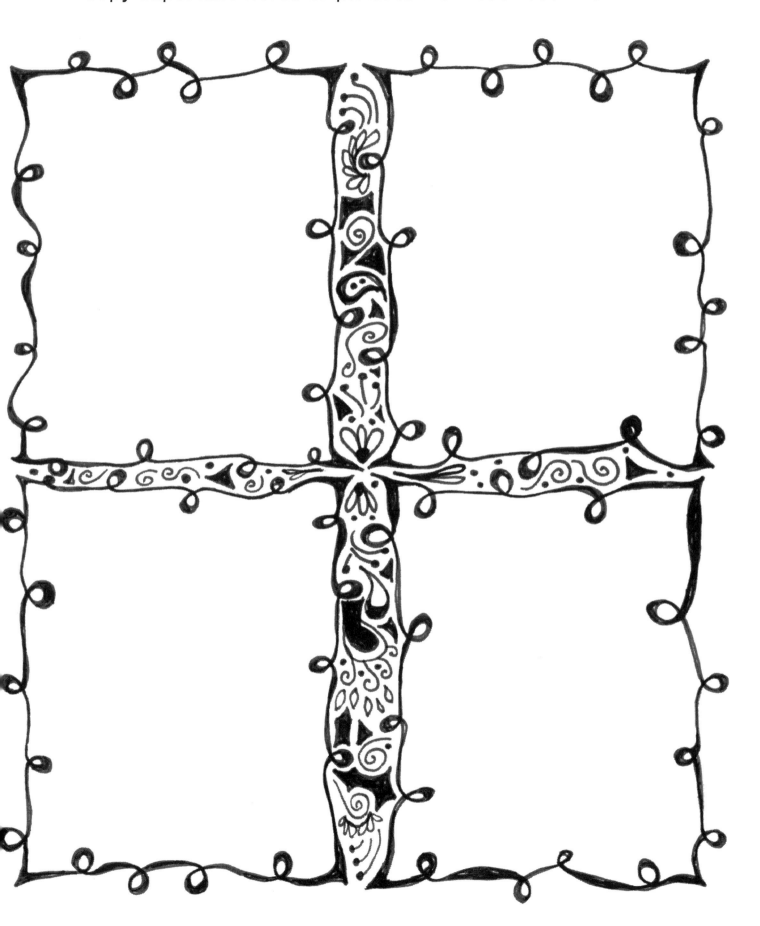

Spelling Time

Find 20 Words with 7 letters each.

Look in your books for words.

Write the words here:

_____   _____

_____   _____

_____   _____

_____   _____

_____   _____

_____   _____

_____   _____

_____   _____

_____   _____

_____   _____

Start Time:

_ _ _ _ _

Stop Time:

_ _ _ _ _

Screen Time!

Watch a Documentary, Educational Program, Movie, or Tutorial.

TITLE: _____

SUBJECT_____

LOCATION:_____

MESSAGE: _____

_____

Rating:

AWFUL

BAD

LAME

YUCKY

OKAY

NICE

GOOD

GREAT

SUPER

AMAZING

Draw a Scene from the video:

Notes:

TITLE:

Use THIS PAGE for Math Practice
Or be creative and design something, like a house! You could make graphs, maps or geometric designs with this graph paper.

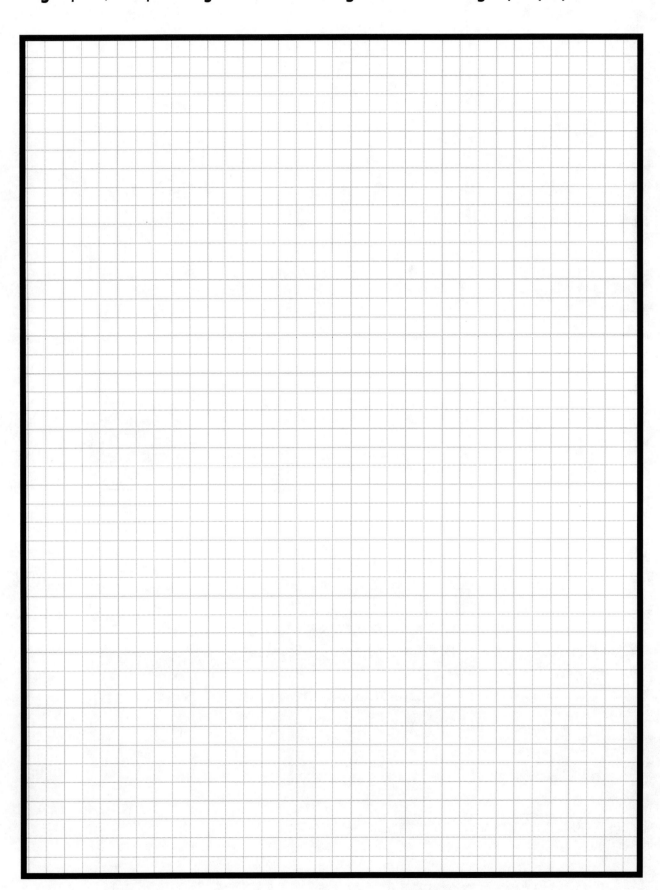

Fun Writing Practice:

ABCDEFGHIJKLMNOPQURSTUVWXYZ

abcdefghijklmnopqrstuvwxyz

ABCDEFGHIJKLMNOPQURSTUVWXYZ

ABCDEFGHIJKLMNOPQURSTUVWXYZ

abcdefghijklmnopqrstuvwxyz

Creative Writing & Copywork

Stories, Poems, Lists and More.

That's what this page is waiting for!

_____

_____

_____

_____

_____

_____

_____

_____

_____

_____

_____

_____

_____

_____

_____

_____

_____

_____

_____

_____

Draw Anything!

Circle Today's Date

January
February
March
April
May
June
July
August
September
October
November
December

1 2 3 4 5 6
7 8 9 10 11
12 13 14 15
16 17 18 19
20 21 22 23
24 25 26 27
28 29 30 31

MONDAY
TUESDAY
WEDNESDAY
THURSDAY
FRIDAY
SATURDAY
SUNDAY

2015
2016
2017
2018
2019
2020
2021
2022
2023
2024
2025
2026
2027
2028
2029

Write Today's Date:_ _ _ _ _ _ _ _ _ _ _ _ _ _

Start Your Day!

Draw Your Dreams:

To-Do List

_____
_____
_____
_____
_____
_____
_____

Picture Study

Look closely at this picture.
Think about the lines and shadows.
Practice working with your colored pencils.

Draw the Missing Spot

Use a variety of smooth black drawing pens,
with fine points, to complete the picture.

Nature Study

Go outside and make a realistic
drawing of something
you find in nature.

Reading Time - 1 Hour (Set a Timer)

Choose Four Books - Read from each book for 15 minutes.

Copy important words or pictures from each book here:

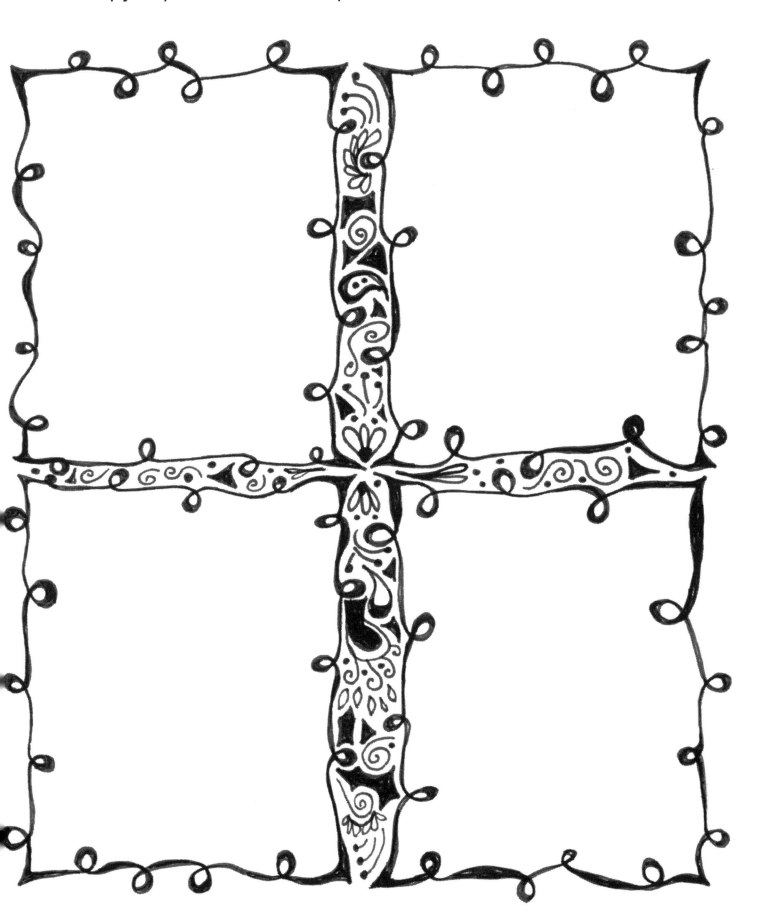

Spelling Time

Find 20 Words with 6 letters each.

Look in your books for words.

Write the words here:

_____   _____

_____   _____

_____   _____

_____   _____

_____   _____

_____   _____

_____   _____

_____   _____

_____   _____

Start Time:

Stop Time:

Screen Time!

Watch a Documentary, Educational Program, Movie, or Tutorial.

TITLE: _____

SUBJECT_____

LOCATION: _____

MESSAGE: _____

_____

Rating:

AWFUL

BAD

LAME

YUCKY

OKAY

NICE

GOOD

GREAT

SUPER

AMAZING

Notes:

TITLE:

Draw a Scene from the video:

Use THIS PAGE for Math Practice

Or be creative and design something, like a house! You could make graphs, maps or geometric designs with this graph paper.

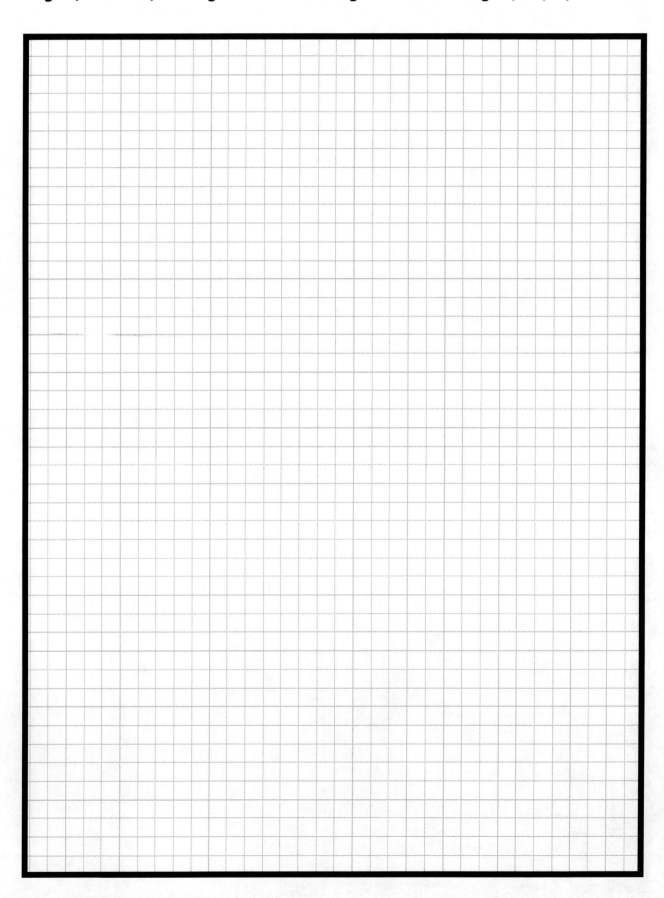

Creative Writing & Copywork

Stories, Poems, Lists and More.

That's what this page is waiting for!

_____

_____

_____

_____

_____

_____

_____

_____

_____

_____

_____

_____

_____

_____

_____

_____

_____

_____

Circle Today's Date

January
February
March
April
May
June
July
August
September
October
November
December

1 2 3 4 5 6
7 8 9 10 11
12 13 14 15
16 17 18 19
20 21 22 23
24 25 26 27
28 29 30 31

MONDAY
TUESDAY
WEDNESDAY
THURSDAY
FRIDAY
SATURDAY
SUNDAY

2015
2016
2017
2018
2019
2020
2021
2022
2023
2024
2025
2026
2027
2028
2029

Write Today's Date: _ _ _ _ _ _ _ _ _ _ _ _ _ _ _

Start Your Day!

Draw Your Dreams:

To-Do List

_____
_____
_____
_____
_____
_____
_____

Picture Study

Look closely at this picture.

Think about the lines and shadows.

Practice working with your colored pencils.

Draw the Missing Spot

Use a variety of smooth black drawing pens,
with fine points, to complete the picture.

Nature Study

Go outside and make a realistic
drawing of something
you find in nature.

Reading Time - 1 Hour (Set a Timer)

Choose Four Books - Read from each book for 15 minutes.

Copy important words or pictures from each book here:

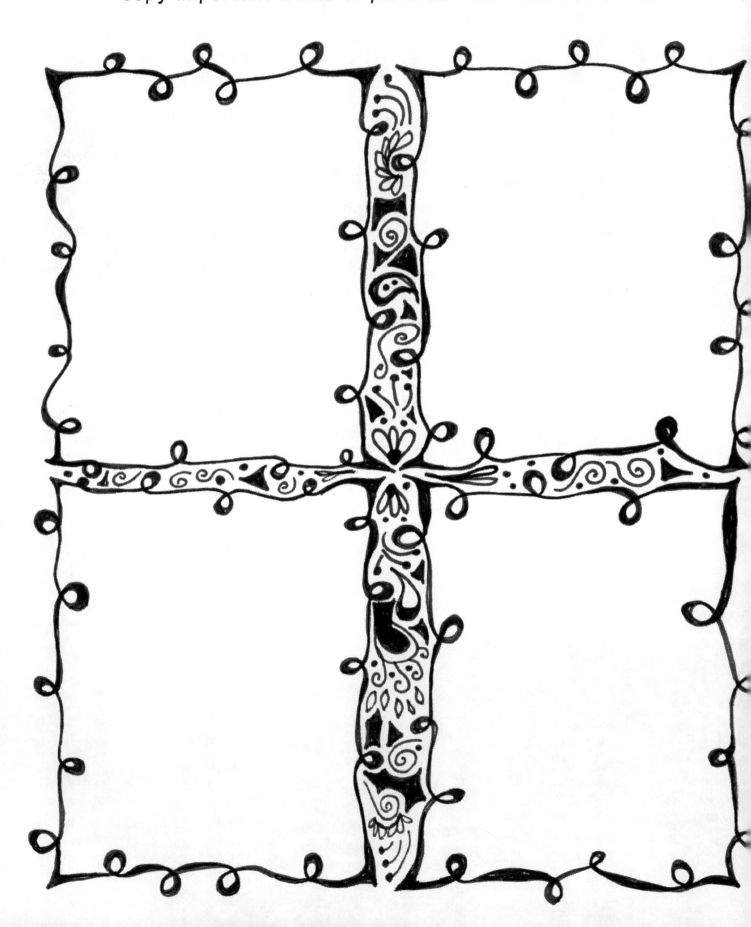

Spelling Time

Find 20 Words with 5 letters each.

Look in your books for words.

Write the words here:

_____   _____

_____   _____

_____   _____

_____   _____

_____   _____

_____   _____

_____   _____

_____   _____

Start Time:

Stop Time:

Screen Time!

Watch a Documentary, Educational Program, Movie, or Tutorial.

TITLE: _____

SUBJECT_____

LOCATION:_____

MESSAGE: _____

_____

Rating:

AWFUL

BAD

LAME

YUCKY

OKAY

NICE

GOOD

GREAT

SUPER

AMAZING

Draw a Scene from the video:

Notes:

TITLE:

Use THIS PAGE for Math Practice

Or be creative and design something, like a house! You could make graphs, maps or geometric designs with this graph paper.

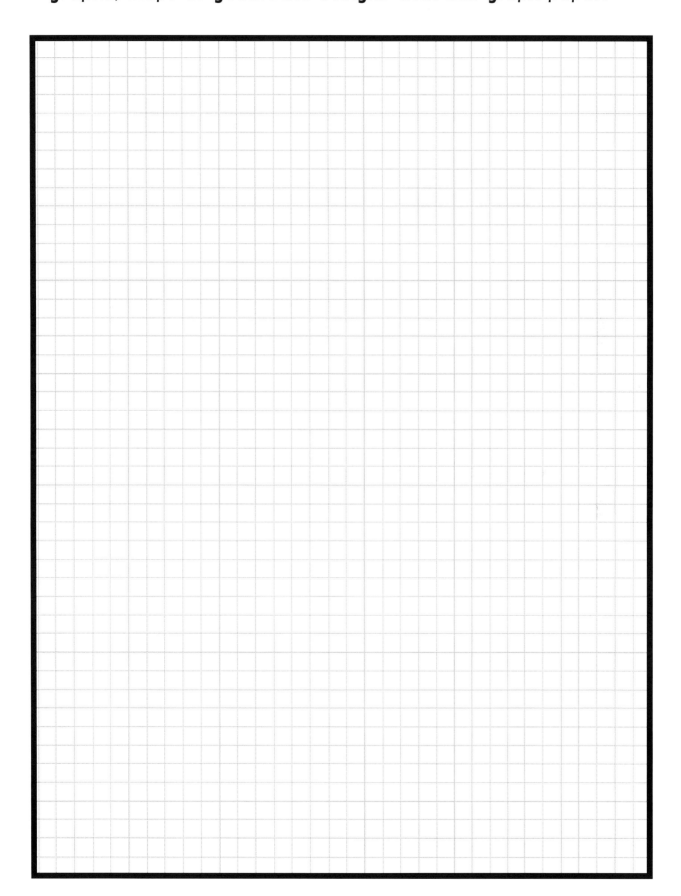

World News Today!

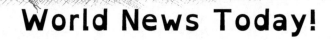

Talk to your parents about current events.

Look at a newspaper, news broadcast or website.

Color the countries you learn about.

Tell the news stories with words or pictures.

Creative Writing & Copywork

Stories, Poems, Lists and More.

That's what this page is waiting for!

_____

_____

_____

_____

_____

_____

_____

_____

_____

_____

_____

_____

_____

_____

_____

_____

_____

_____

Draw Anything!

Circle Today's Date

January
February
March
April
May
June
July
August
September
October
November
December

1 2 3 4 5 6
7 8 9 10 11
12 13 14 15
16 17 18 19
20 21 22 23
24 25 26 27
28 29 30 31

MONDAY
TUESDAY
WEDNESDAY
THURSDAY
FRIDAY
SATURDAY
SUNDAY

2015
2016
2017
2018
2019
2020
2021
2022
2023
2024
2025
2026
2027
2028
2029

Write Today's Date: _ _ _ _ _ _ _ _ _ _ _ _ _ _ _ _ _ _ _

Start Your Day!

Draw Your Dreams:

To-Do List

_____

_____

_____

_____

_____

_____

_____

Nature Study

Go outside and make a realistic
drawing of something
you find in nature.

Reading Time - 1 Hour (Set a Timer)

Choose Four Books - Read from each book for 15 minutes.

Copy important words or pictures from each book here:

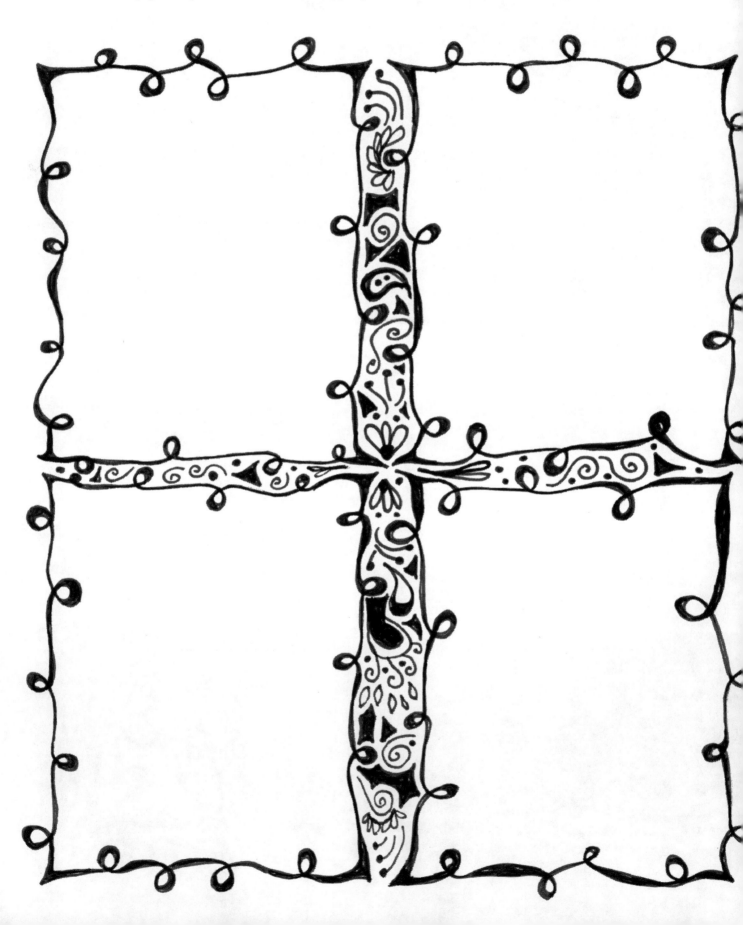

Spelling Time

Find 20 Words with 6 letters each.

Look in your books for words.

Write the words here:

_____   _____

_____   _____

_____   _____

_____   _____

_____   _____

_____   _____

_____   _____

_____   _____

_____   _____

_____   _____

Start Time:

_____

Stop Time:

_____

Screen Time!

Watch a Documentary, Educational Program, Movie, or Tutorial.

TITLE: _____

SUBJECT _____

LOCATION: _____

MESSAGE: _____

_____

Rating:

AWFUL

BAD

LAME

YUCKY

OKAY

NICE

GOOD

GREAT

SUPER

AMAZING

Draw a Scene from the video:

Notes:

TITLE:

Use THIS PAGE for Math Practice

Or be creative and design something, like a house! You could make graphs, maps or geometric designs with this graph paper.

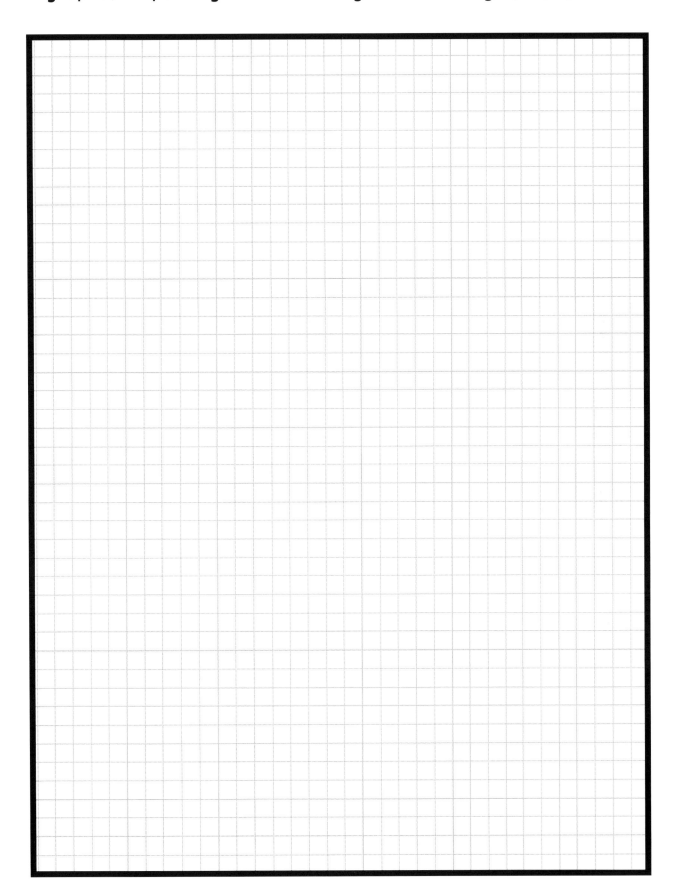

Listening Time

Listen to an audio book or classical music or ask someone to read a story to you while you color and draw on the next page.

What are you listening to?

_____

Draw Anything!

Circle Today's Date

January
February
March
April
May
June
July
August
September
October
November
December

1 2 3 4 5 6
7 8 9 10 11
12 13 14 15
16 17 18 19
20 21 22 23
24 25 26 27
28 29 30 31

MONDAY
TUESDAY
WEDNESDAY
THURSDAY
FRIDAY
SATURDAY
SUNDAY

2015
2016
2017
2018
2019
2020
2021
2022
2023
2024
2025
2026
2027
2028
2029

Write Today's Date:_ _ _ _ _ _ _ _ _ _ _ _ _ _ _

Start Your Day!

Draw Your Dreams:

To-Do List

_____
_____
_____
_____
_____
_____
_____

Picture Study

Look closely at this picture.

Think about the lines and shadows.

Practice working with your colored pencils.

Draw the Missing Spot

Use a variety of smooth black drawing pens,
with fine points, to complete the picture.

Nature Study

Go outside and make a realistic
drawing of something
you find in nature.

Reading Time - 1 Hour (Set a Timer)
Choose Four Books - Read from each book for 15 minutes.
Copy important words or pictures from each book here:

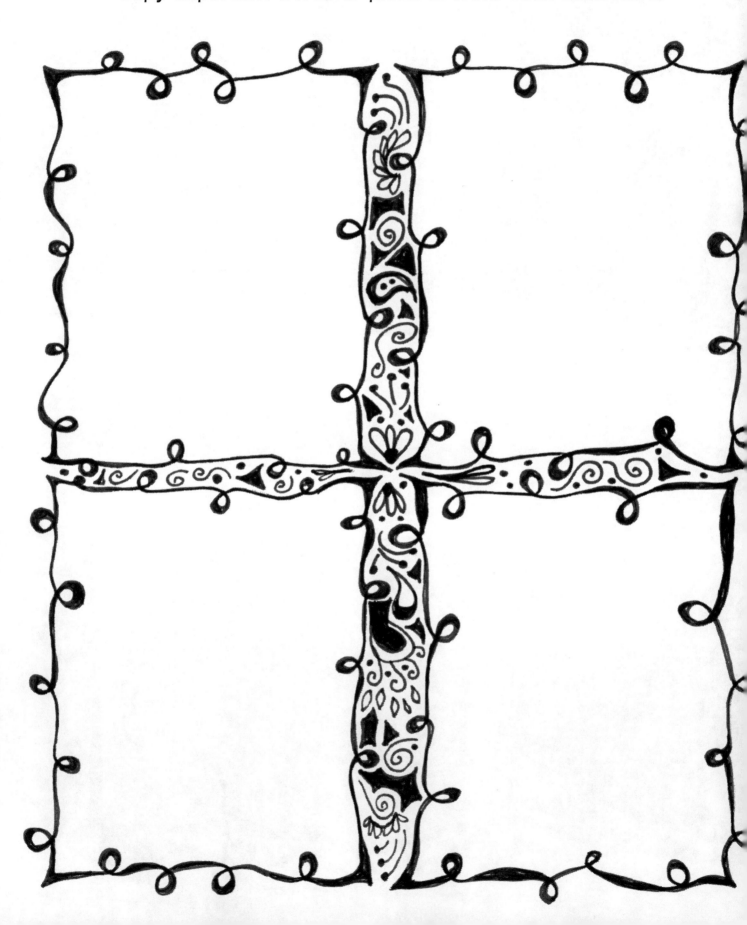

Spelling Time

Find 20 Words with 7 letters each.
Look in your books for words.
Write the words here:

_____   _____

_____   _____

_____   _____

_____   _____

_____   _____

_____   _____

_____   _____

_____   _____

_____   _____

Start Time:

_ _ _ _ _

Stop Time:

_ _ _ _ _

Screen Time!

Watch a Documentary, Educational Program, Movie, or Tutorial.

TITLE: _____

SUBJECT_____

LOCATION:_____

MESSAGE: _____

_____

Rating:

AWFUL

BAD

LAME

YUCKY

OKAY

NICE

GOOD

GREAT

SUPER

AMAZING

Draw a Scene from the video:

Notes:

TITLE:

Use THIS PAGE for Math Practice

Or be creative and design something, like a house! You could make graphs, maps or geometric designs with this graph paper.

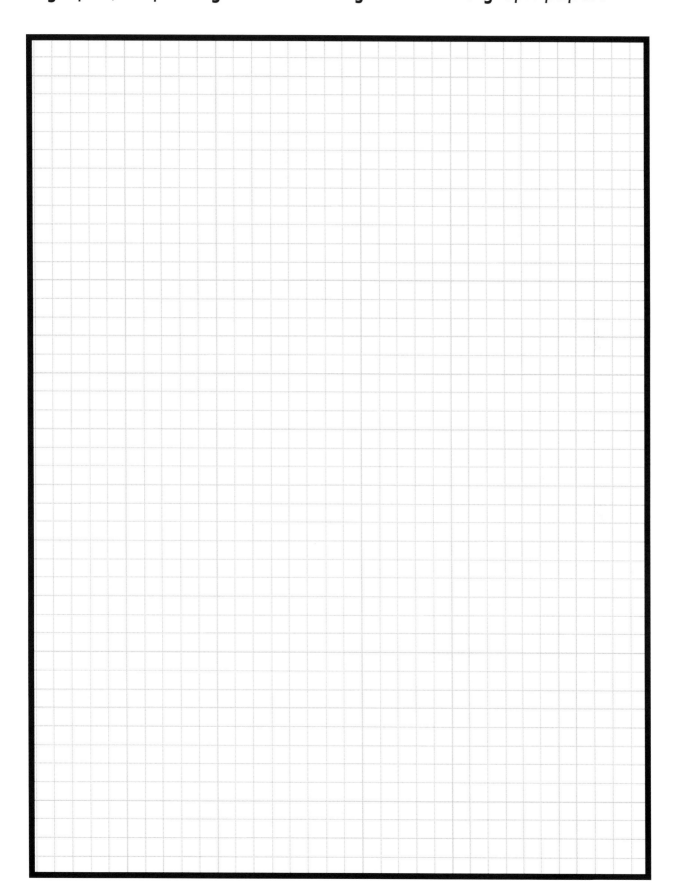

Fun Writing Practice:

ABCDEFGHIJKLMNOPQURSTUVWXYZ

abcdefghijklmnopqrstuvwxyz

ABCDEFGHIJKLMNOPQURSTUVWXYZ

ABCDEFGHIJKLMNOPQURSTUVWXYZ

abcdefghijklmnopqrstuvwxyz

Creative Writing & Copywork

Stories, Poems, Lists and More.

That's what this page is waiting for!

_____

_____

_____

_____

_____

_____

_____

_____

_____

_____

_____

_____

_____

_____

_____

_____

_____

_____

Draw Anything!

Circle Today's Date

January
February
March
April
May
June
July
August
September
October
November
December

1 2 3 4 5 6
7 8 9 10 11
12 13 14 15
16 17 18 19
20 21 22 23
24 25 26 27
28 29 30 31

MONDAY
TUESDAY
WEDNESDAY
THURSDAY
FRIDAY
SATURDAY
SUNDAY

2015
2016
2017
2018
2019
2020
2021
2022
2023
2024
2025
2026
2027
2028
2029

Write Today's Date:_ _ _ _ _ _ _ _ _ _ _ _ _ _

Start Your Day!

Draw Your Dreams:

To-Do List

_____
_____
_____
_____
_____
_____
_____

Nature Study

Go outside and make a realistic
drawing of something
you find in nature.

Reading Time - 1 Hour (Set a Timer)

Choose Four Books - Read from each book for 15 minutes.

Copy important words or pictures from each book here:

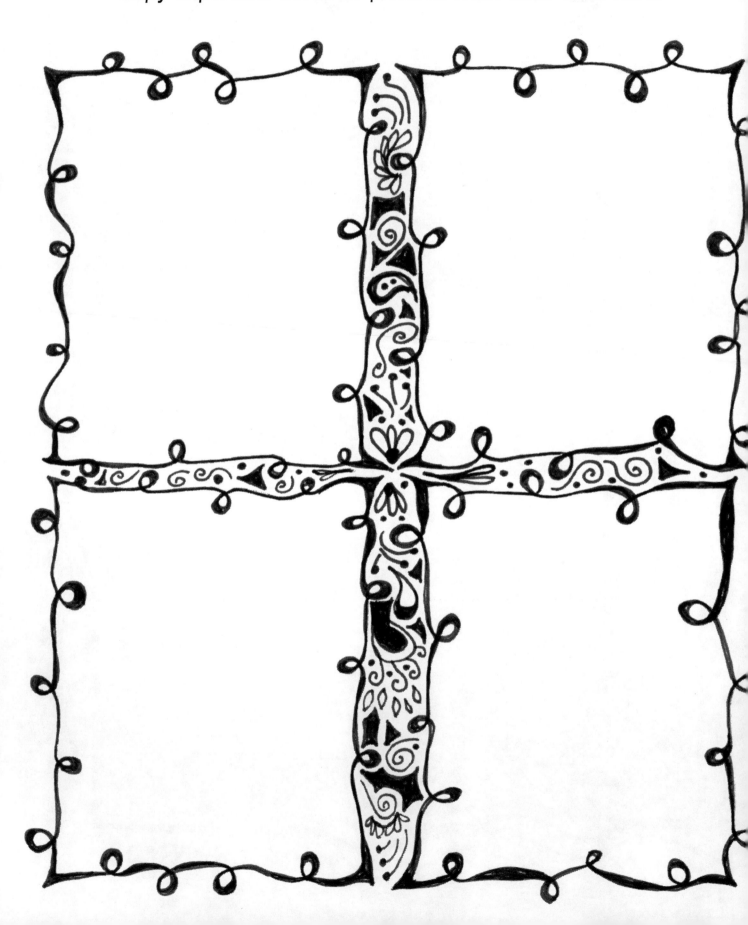

Spelling Time

Find 20 Words with 8 letters each.

Look in your books for words.

Write the words here:

Start
Time:

_ _ _ _ _

Stop
Time:

_ _ _ _ _

Screen
Time!

Watch a
Documentary,
Educational
Program,
Movie, or
Tutorial.

TITLE: _____

SUBJECT_____

LOCATION:_____

MESSAGE: _____

_____

Rating:

AWFUL

BAD

LAME

YUCKY

OKAY

NICE

GOOD

GREAT

SUPER

AMAZING

Notes:

TITLE:

Draw a Scene from the video:

Use THIS PAGE for Math Practice

Or be creative and design something, like a house! You could make graphs, maps or geometric designs with this graph paper.

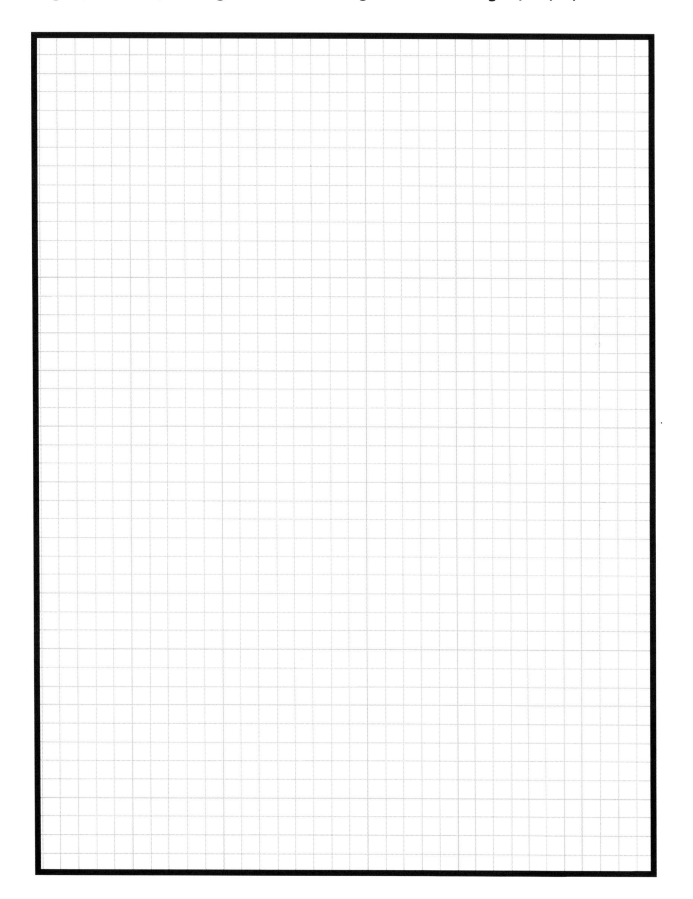

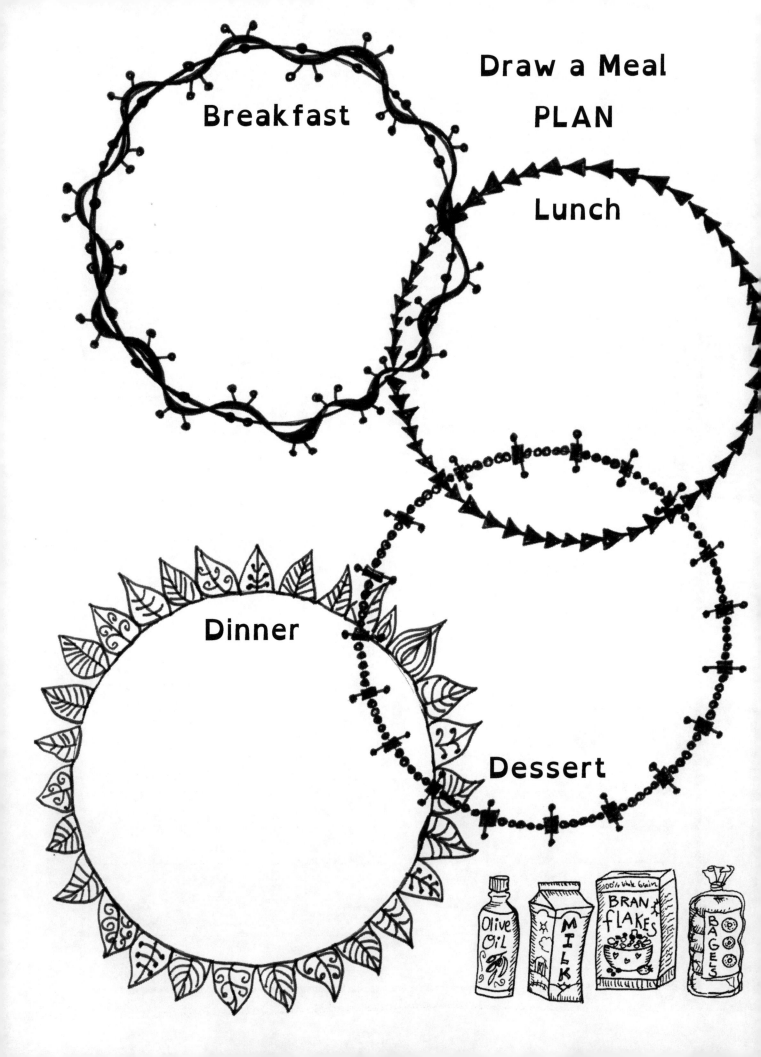

Creative Writing & Copywork

Stories, Poems, Lists and More.
That's what this page is waiting for!

_____

_____

_____

_____

_____

_____

_____

_____

_____

_____

_____

_____

_____

_____

_____

_____

_____

My FUN Page

Circle Today's Date

January
February
March
April
May
June
July
August
September
October
November
December

1 2 3 4 5 6
7 8 9 10 11
12 13 14 15
16 17 18 19
20 21 22 23
24 25 26 27
28 29 30 31

MONDAY
TUESDAY
WEDNESDAY
THURSDAY
FRIDAY
SATURDAY
SUNDAY

2015
2016
2017
2018
2019
2020
2021
2022
2023
2024
2025
2026
2027
2028
2029

Write Today's Date: _ _ _ _ _ _ _ _ _ _ _ _ _ _ _ _

Start Your Day!

Draw Your Dreams:

To-Do List

_____
_____
_____
_____
_____
_____
_____

Picture Study

Look closely at this picture.

Think about the lines and shadows.

Practice working with your colored pencils.

Draw the Missing Spot

Use a variety of smooth black drawing pens,
with fine points, to complete the picture.

Nature Study

Go outside and make a realistic
drawing of something
you find in nature.

Reading Time - 1 Hour (Set a Timer)

Choose Four Books - Read from each book for 15 minutes.

Copy important words or pictures from each book here:

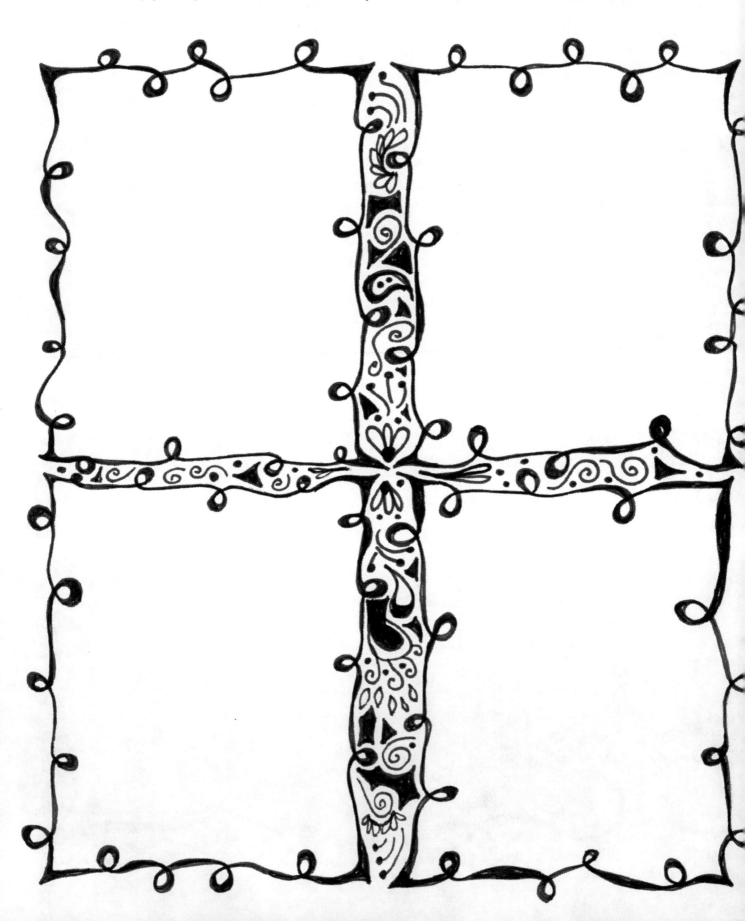

Spelling Time

Find 20 Words with 7 letters each.

Look in your books for words.

Write the words here:

_____   _____

_____   _____

_____   _____

_____   _____

_____   _____

_____   _____

_____   _____

_____   _____

_____   _____

Start Time:

_ _ _ _ _

Stop Time:

_ _ _ _ _

Screen Time!

Watch a Documentary, Educational Program, Movie, or Tutorial.

TITLE: _____

SUBJECT _____

LOCATION: _____

MESSAGE: _____

_____

Rating:

AWFUL

BAD

LAME

YUCKY

OKAY

NICE

GOOD

GREAT

SUPER

AMAZING

Notes:

TITLE:

Draw a Scene from the video:

Use THIS PAGE for Math Practice

Or be creative and design something, like a house! You could make graphs, maps or geometric designs with this graph paper.

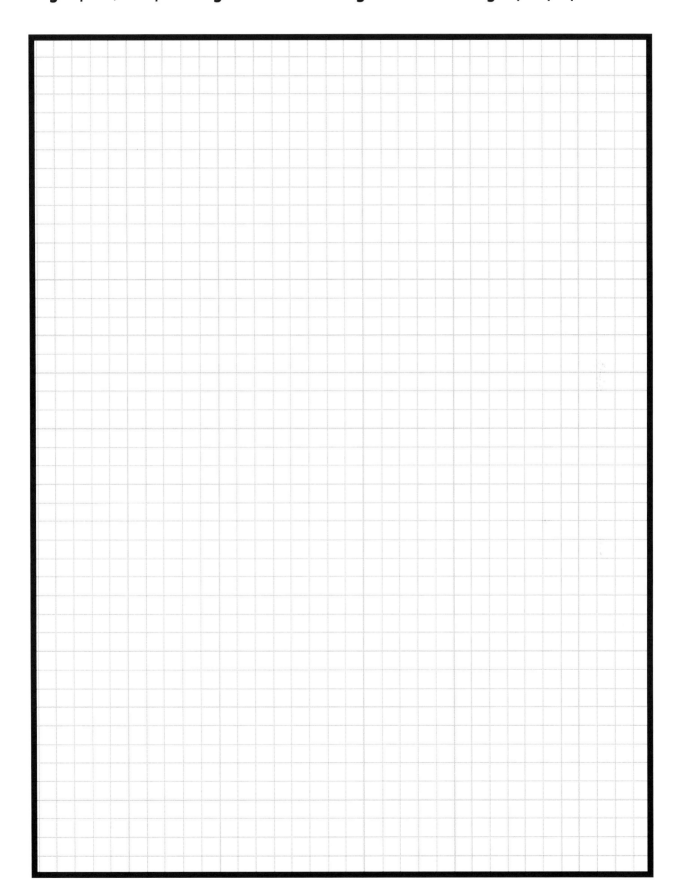

Creative Writing & Copywork

Stories, Poems, Lists and More.

That's what this page is waiting for!

_____

_____

_____

_____

_____

_____

_____

_____

_____

_____

_____

_____

_____

_____

_____

_____

_____

Draw Anything!

Circle Today's Date

January
February
March
April
May
June
July
August
September
October
November
December

1 2 3 4 5 6
7 8 9 10 11
12 13 14 15
16 17 18 19
20 21 22 23
24 25 26 27
28 29 30 31

MONDAY
TUESDAY
WEDNESDAY
THURSDAY
FRIDAY
SATURDAY
SUNDAY

2015
2016
2017
2018
2019
2020
2021
2022
2023
2024
2025
2026
2027
2028
2029

Write Today's Date: _ _ _ _ _ _ _ _ _ _ _ _ _

Start Your Day!

Draw Your Dreams:

To-Do List

_____
_____
_____
_____
_____
_____
_____

Nature Study

Go outside and make a realistic
drawing of something
you find in nature.

Reading Time - 1 Hour (Set a Timer)

Choose Four Books - Read from each book for 15 minutes.

Copy important words or pictures from each book here:

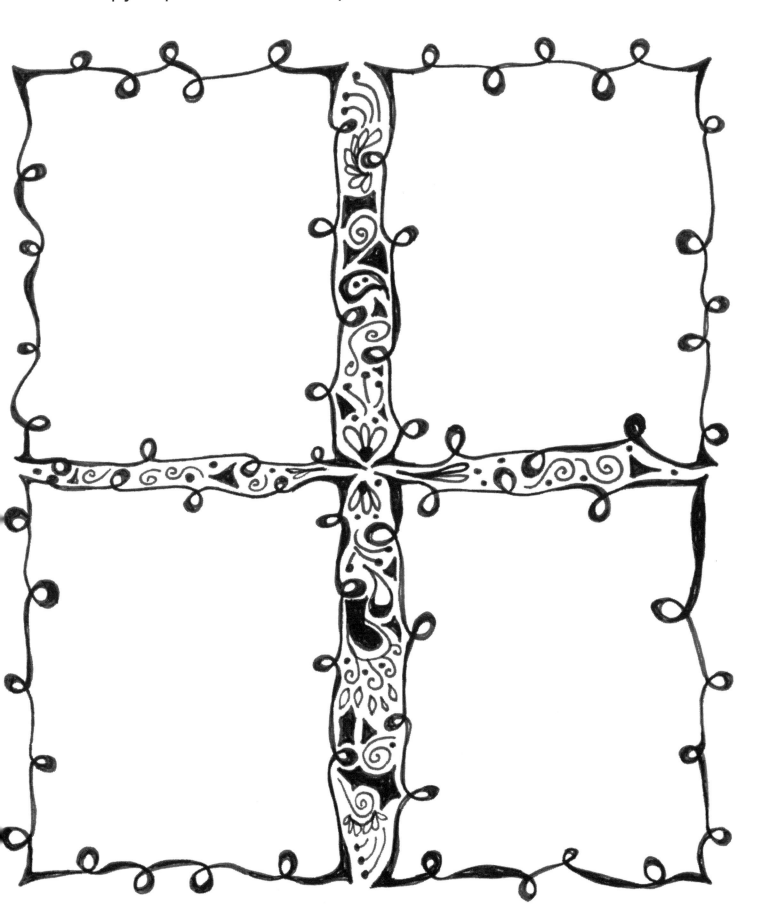

Spelling Time

Find 20 Words with **7** letters each.
Look in your books for words.
Write the words here:

_____   _____

_____   _____

_____   _____

_____   _____

_____   _____

_____   _____

_____   _____

_____   _____

_____   _____

_____   _____

Screen Time!

Watch a Documentary, Educational Program, Movie, or Tutorial.

Start Time: _____

Stop Time: _____

TITLE: _____

SUBJECT _____

LOCATION: _____

MESSAGE: _____

_____

Rating:
AWFUL
BAD
LAME
YUCKY
OKAY
NICE
GOOD
GREAT
SUPER
AMAZING

Draw a Scene from the video:

Notes:

TITLE:

Use THIS PAGE for Math Practice

Or be creative and design something, like a house! You could make graphs, maps or geometric designs with this graph paper.

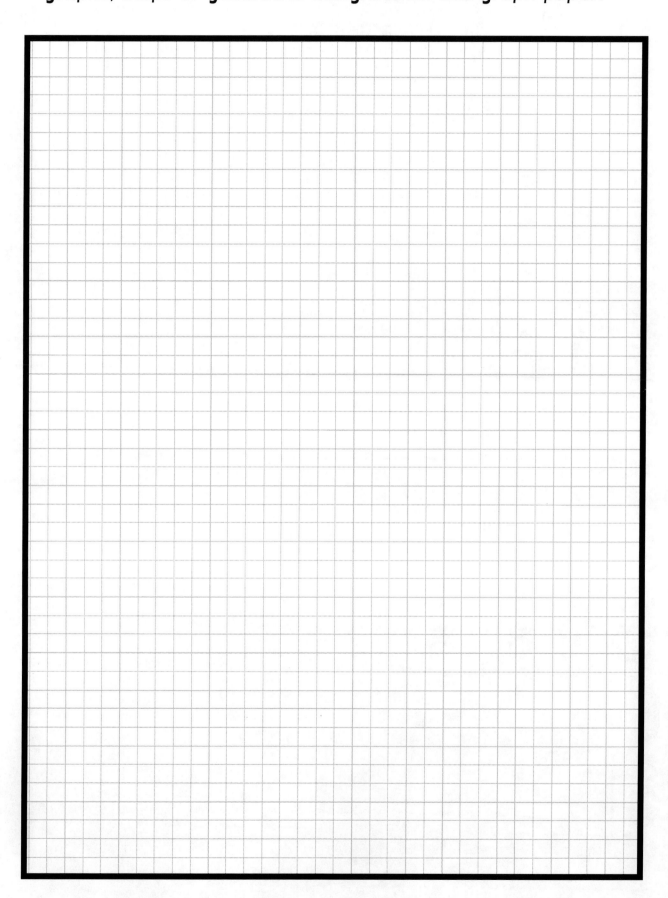

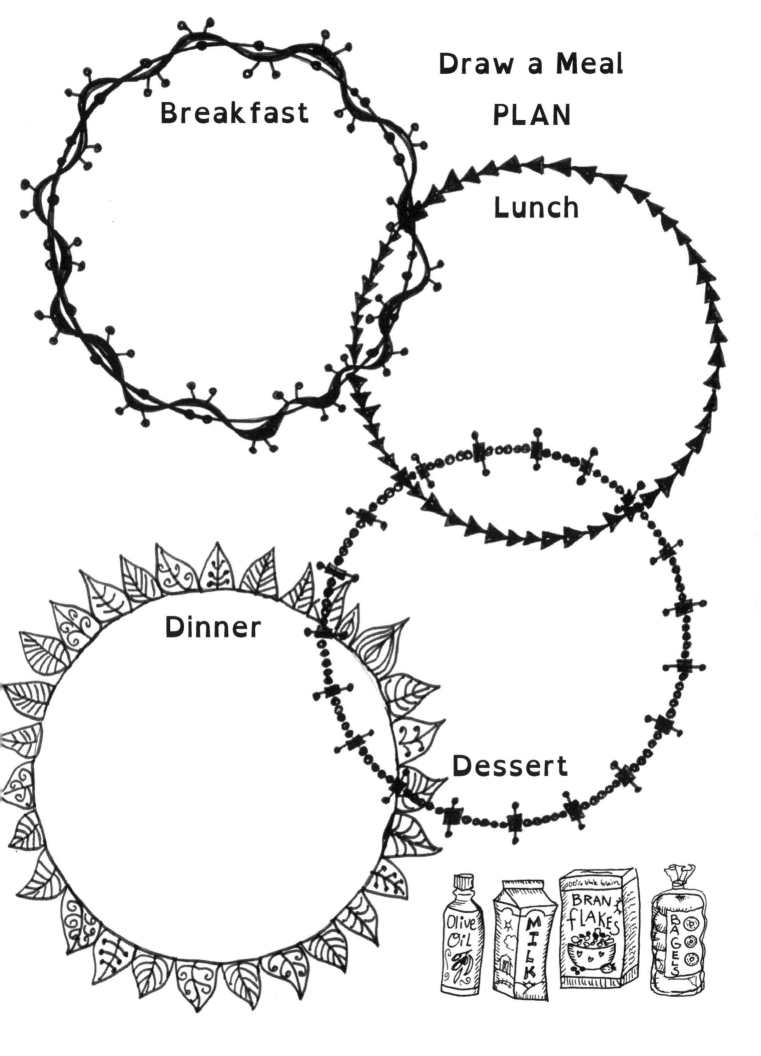

Creative Writing & Copywork

Stories, Poems, Lists and More.

That's what this page is waiting for!

_____

_____

_____

_____

_____

_____

_____

_____

_____

_____

_____

_____

_____

_____

_____

_____

_____

_____

Draw Anything!

Circle Today's Date

January
February
March
April
May
June
July
August
September
October
November
December

1 2 3 4 5 6
7 8 9 10 11
12 13 14 15
16 17 18 19
20 21 22 23
24 25 26 27
28 29 30 31

MONDAY
TUESDAY
WEDNESDAY
THURSDAY
FRIDAY
SATURDAY
SUNDAY

2015
2016
2017
2018
2019
2020
2021
2022
2023
2024
2025
2026
2027
2028
2029

Write Today's Date:_ _ _ _ _ _ _ _ _ _ _ _ _

Start Your Day!

Draw Your Dreams:

To-Do List

_____

_____

_____

_____

_____

_____

_____

Picture Study

Look closely at this picture.

Think about the lines and shadows.

Practice working with your colored pencils.

Draw the Missing Spot

Use a variety of smooth black drawing pens,
with fine points, to complete the picture.

Nature Study

Go outside and make a realistic
drawing of something
you find in nature.

Reading Time - 1 Hour (Set a Timer)

Choose Four Books - Read from each book for 15 minutes.

Copy important words or pictures from each book here:

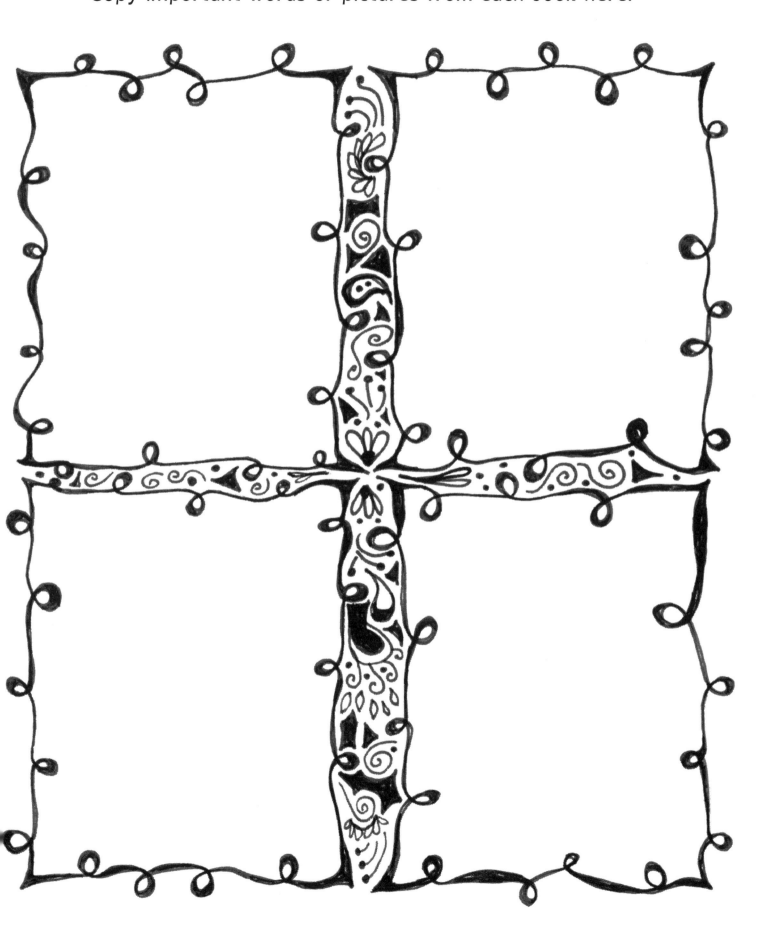

Spelling Time

Find 20 Words with 10 letters each.

Look in your books for words.

Write the words here:

_____   _____

_____   _____

_____   _____

_____   _____

_____   _____

_____   _____

_____   _____

_____   _____

_____   _____

_____   _____

Start Time:

_____

Stop Time:

_____

Screen Time!

Watch a Documentary, Educational Program, Movie, or Tutorial.

TITLE: _____

SUBJECT_____

LOCATION:_____

MESSAGE: _____

_____

Notes:

Draw a Scene from the video:

Rating:

AWFUL

BAD

LAME

YUCKY

OKAY

NICE

GOOD

GREAT

SUPER

AMAZING

Use THIS PAGE for Math Practice
Or be creative and design something, like a house! You could make graphs, maps or geometric designs with this graph paper.

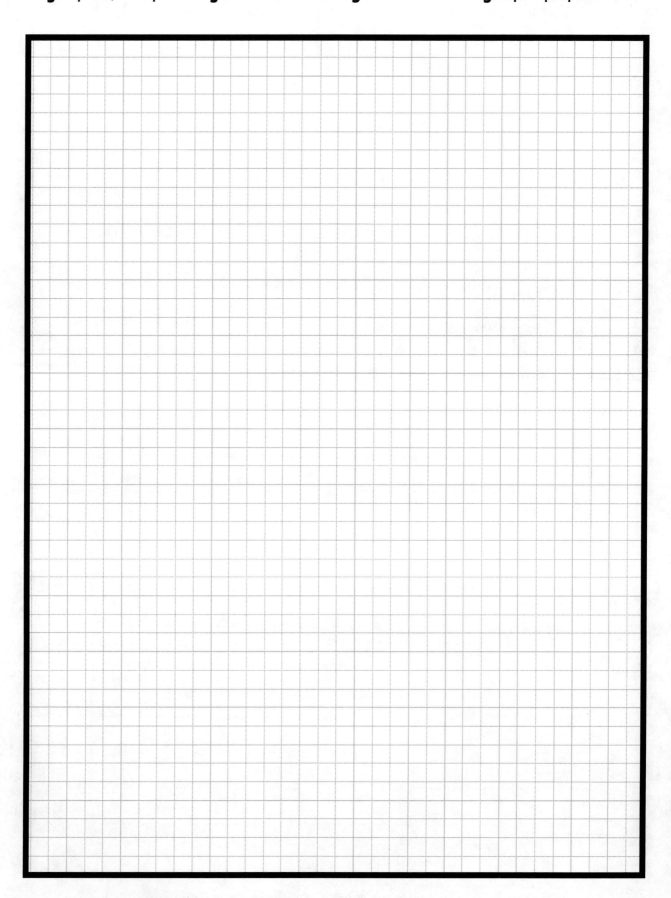

Creative Writing & Copywork

Stories, Poems, Lists and More.
That's what this page is waiting for!

_____

_____

_____

_____

_____

_____

_____

_____

_____

_____

_____

_____

_____

_____

_____

_____

_____

_____

Draw Anything!

Draw Anything!

Draw Anything!

My FUN Page

My FUN Page

My FUN Page

My FUN Page

My FUN Page

Do It Yourself
HOMESCHOOL
JOURNALS

Copyright Information

Contact Us:

The Thinking Tree LLC
617 N. Swope St. Greenfield, IN 46140. United States
317.622.8852 PHONE (Dial +1 outside of the USA) 267.712.7889 FAX
www.DyslexiaGames.com
jbrown@DyslexiaGames.com

My FUN Page

Made in United States
Orlando, FL
10 September 2024